COCKTAIL
AMERICA

OVER 200 COCKTAILS FROM AMERICA'S GREATEST CITIES

★

CIDER MILL PRESS

BOOK PUBLISHERS

COCKTAIL AMERICA

ISBN-13: 978-1-40034-062-0
ISBN-10: 1-40034-062-4

This book may be ordered by mail from the publisher. Please include $5.99 for postage and handling. Please support your local bookseller first!

Books published by Cider Mill Press Book Publishers are available at special discounts for bulk purchases in the United States by corporations, institutions, and other organizations. For more information, please contact the publisher.

Cider Mill Press Book Publishers
"Where good books are ready for press"
501 Nelson Place
Nashville, Tennessee 37214
cidermillpress.com

Typography: Modesto Expanded, Modesto Poster, Avenir, Copperplate, Sackers, Warnock

Image Credits: Pages 3, 4–5, 12–13, 78–79, 172–173, 183, 210–211, 252–253, 282–283, 412–413 used under official license from Shutterstock. All other photos courtesy of Cider Mill Press.

Printed in Malaysia

24 25 26 27 28 COS 5 4 3 2 1

First Edition

CONTENTS

INTRODUCTION

L ong-held beliefs die hard.

There are no doubt plenty of places around the globe where any suggestion that the bars in America are on the same level as the mixological meccas operating in places like London, Paris, Berlin, Tokyo, and Hong Kong would be met with derisive laughter and a swift dismissal.

Such an inclination is no doubt tied to the well-worn picture of America that has been passed around the world—in it sit a group of rowdy beer-slugging drinkers, crowding around the bar at a chain restaurant, screaming themselves crimson over whatever is happening in the football game.

And, to avoid any confusion, we're talking SEC or NFL rather than Premier League, or Bundesliga.

Of course, there are spots around the country where these superior folks could go and find evidence that supported their disdainful stance.

But, should you draw their attention to the cocktail menu at the very establishment where they went to make their case, they will almost assuredly find signs that the contemporary cocktail revolution has become so successful in the United States that even the most middlebrow places have incorporated elements of it, with well-thought-out, carefully constructed drinks featuring once fantastical ingredients like mezcal, amaro, and housemade herbal syrups now commonplace all over the country.

Having blown their minds with that exhibition, ask them to just imagine what's going on in cosmopolitan cities like New York, Miami, and LA, and what is being dreamed up in the country's hotbeds of culinary creativity, like San Francisco and Portland (both Oregon and Maine).

Now that they have been taken down from their high horse, it's time for the coup de grâce—slide the list of the World's 50 Best Bars in front of them, and they'll see that five U.S. establishments made it in 2023.

And all of these indications are just the tip of the iceberg—by any measure, America is in fact a cocktail kingdom.

For the cocktail as the world now knows it actually began with a New York bartender named Jerry Thomas. The owner and operator of saloons across the country during the nineteenth century, Thomas somehow found some time to collect all that he had learned in his life behind the bar and create his seminal *Bar-Tender's Guide*. Published in 1862, it was the first drinks book ever printed in the United States, an impressive accomplishment in its own right.

But the legacy of that tome extends well beyond being the first through the door. As the *New York Times* said, "Thomas's book was a revelation. At a time when bartenders relied on powdered mixes, canned fruit juices and a narrow repertory of perhaps a dozen drinks, Thomas imparted a lofty sense of the bartender's vocation." That elevated touch kept Thomas's book in circulation throughout the twentieth century—though its advice, as anyone who frequented a bar in the late 1970s can attest, was not always heeded. Then, just as cocktail culture was at its nadir, came the day in the 1980s when Joe Baum, the then-owner of New York's famed Rainbow Room, handed a copy to his bartender, Dale DeGroff.

The rest is history.

By digging into the details and using trial-and-error to decode Thomas's famously vague prescriptions, DeGroff began to open people's eyes to what a cocktail was capable of. In a true craftsman's hands, it was revealed to be far more than an expedient means of getting booze into one's system. Instead, the preparation of a well-made cocktail became an event, as worthy of care and creativity as any other course a patron would consume during a big night on the town.

In the matter of a few decades, DeGroff had transformed a city that was, in his own words, "a beer and highball, rum and Tab town, then—Chardonnay, a Mimosa or Bloody Mary, maybe you could order a [Sea Breeze] or something made with fake sour mix," when he first started tending bar in the late '60s.

While DeGroff was transforming the Big Apple, others across the country were similarly saving people from the prefabricated mixers, artificial juices, and other commonly used items that are better suited to being used in a car engine than a Tom Collins. There was Lucy Brennan in Portland, Oregon, who contemporary bar star Jeffrey Morgenthaler cites as the wellspring from which that city's rich cocktail culture sprung. Murray Stenson loomed similarly large in Seattle, becoming so popular that his mere presence behind the bar became enough to guarantee a new restaurant success in the brutally competitive service industry, as legions of Murray devotees were assured to pack the place night after night.

From these early passionate few, a revolution flourished. There is now almost no part of the country where a cocktail aficionado has to fear going without a well-made serve being available.

★

As the history of this nation did, our bar-hopping tour of the United States starts in the Northeast. Of course, there will be no shortage of drinks from New York, which is not only the apex of late-night life in this country, but is also, along with London and Tokyo, one of the capitals of the contemporary cocktail renaissance.

But beyond the bright lights of Manhattan—and, now, Brooklyn—there are numerous towns in the Northeast where one could happily spend a week bar hopping, finding a new favorite each day.

Once you've gotten your fill of bar stylings in the Northeast, it's time for us to head down 95 to Washington, D.C., the country's capital. Again, once there we find that the image we may have in our head—lobbyists and other political players sitting around soulless steak houses, smirking at the stupidity of the little people over an endless string of vodka Martinis—is continually overturned and upset.

Florida no doubt brings to mind slushy, boozy beverages, and while that Buffett-inspired image is true of many towns in the Sunshine State, Miami is a different beast, with a scene that proves to be astonishingly good at blending a bevy of influences to produce a cocktail scene that is one of the world's best. Under the guidance of John Lermayer, bartenders in Miami have mastered creating cocktails that are as masterful as they are playful.

After the excitement and energy of Miami, it's time to unwind, take a step back, and let the evening take what shape it may. Luckily, there is perhaps no better city for doing this than our next stop: New Orleans. The birthplace of seminal drinks such as the Sazerac, Grasshopper, Hurricane, and Ramos Gin Fizz, the Big Easy has embedded cocktail hour into the course of a typical day, and, as anyone who has visited there knows, Bourbon Street is just a small slice of that city—there are plenty of spots where craft and camaraderie carry far more weight than crazy antics. Our trip through the South also takes us through America's latest boomtown, Nashville.

Though it is tempting to continue to remain where it's warm, the Midwest is impossible to look past for the cocktail lover. This will not be news to anyone who has ever spent any time there in the summer, but Chicago is, by every meaningful metric, one of the great cities in the world. The Twin Cities, Minneapolis and St. Paul, also have a flourishing cocktail scene, as you will see in the drinks that hail from there—they are some of the best-looking serves in this entire book.

Having enjoyed our time in the heartland, it's time to tackle the mythical land of Texas, where the extreme heat has fostered a strong tradition of refreshers like the Ranch Water (see page 260), Chilton (see page 256), and Frozen Margarita (see page 259), and a serious influx of wealth, dreamers, and hard-nosed creatives has transformed the Lone Star State into a place with a cocktail scene that can back up the bravado of its residents.

The drive across Texas is, to put it mildly, lengthy. And, at times, nerve-wracking. But whenever the remoteness is about to become too much for one's mind, what lies on the other side—the West—is there to supply reassurance. As Hollywood and Silicon Valley have shown, America's Golden Land has enough talent and creativity to lead the entire world, and the cocktail scenes in Los Angeles, San Francisco, and Las Vegas are on a similarly elevated plane. San Francisco in particular shows out here, in part because its history extends slightly further back than most places in the West—Jerry Thomas, the godfather himself, plied his trade there during the Gold Rush—and in part because the bars and bartenders there seem to be focused slightly more on craft than clicks.

When most people think of the city that shifted the culinary world toward artisanal products and a focus on local ingredients, most would cite Brooklyn. But in truth, Seattle and Portland, Oregon, are right there beside that notorious borough, and probably even exceed Brooklyn in terms of enthusiasm for it. Quality and exceptional craftsmanship are by now embedded into the cultures of those two cities, and that goes double for their bar scenes.

The tour ends there, but do not fret—this book makes it easy to visit your favorite spot any time you need to get away.

NORTHEAST

Amelia ★ Periodista

New York Sour ★ Algorithm of the Night

Turmeric & Tequila ★ Orchard Rita

Forth & Clyde ★ Ship, Captain, Crew

Gin-Gin Mule ★ Leave It to Me (No. 2)

Crown Spritz ★ Mango Caipirinha

Haitian Divorce ★ Pineapple | Vetiver

Blood, Lust & Diamonds ★ Fear Factor

Tia Mia ★ Neon God ★ Oaxaca Old Fashioned

Spirited Away ★ Naked & Famous

Flirtbird ★ Dauphin ★ Joy Division

Mace ★ The Escape ★ Lawyers, Guns & Money

Gins & Roses ★ Third Player

Lost in Translation

Our pub crawl around the country starts in the very same place the nation did—the Northeast. As you might imagine, there will be no shortage of drinks from New York, which is not only the apex of late-night life in this country, but is also, along with London and Tokyo, one of the capitals of the contemporary cocktail renaissance.

In the late 1990s and early 2000s, bars like Audrey Saunders's Pegu Club and Sasha Petraske's Milk & Honey elevated what the cocktail was capable of, and when Death & Co showed up in 2006, the mixological revolution that is now in evidence all over the country began in earnest.

But beyond the bright lights of Manhattan—and, now, Brooklyn—there are numerous towns in the region for the cocktail connoisseur to keep an eye on. Dubious? Just take a spin through the shallow cross-section we've taken from Portland, Maine. Yes, it's a town of just 60,000. But natural beauty, a period of affordable rent (it's now, like seemingly everywhere, astronomical), and a steady influx of super-creative folks have combined to produce one of the country's best culinary cities, and it isn't just us who thinks so—*Bon Appétit* named it Restaurant City of the Year in 2018. As you'll see, bars like Blyth & Burrows are more than keeping pace with the best restaurants there in terms of quality and creativity. Even Boston, whose pugnacious, pub-dwelling, rabid sports fans have likely done much to color the image of American drinking culture around the globe, has benefitted from the rising tide, reliably fashioning cocktails that are accessible yet elegant.

AMELIA

EMPLOYEES ONLY
NEW YORK, NEW YORK

Originally opened in 2004 by a team of industry friends—Dushan Zaric, Henry LaFargue, Igor Hadzismajlovic, Jason Kosmas, and Bill Gilroy—Employees Only has since opened outposts around the world, including Miami and Singapore. It's a great place to find exquisite food and drink, like this romantic cocktail created by Kosmas.

★

GLASSWARE: Coupe
GARNISH: Fresh mint

- 1½ oz. vodka
- 1 oz. Blackberry Puree (see recipe)
- ¾ oz. St-Germain
- ½ oz. fresh lemon juice

1. Chill the coupe in the freezer.
2. Place all of the ingredients in a cocktail shaker, fill it two-thirds of the way with ice, and shake until chilled.
3. Strain the cocktail into the chilled coupe, garnish with fresh mint, and enjoy.

BLACKBERRY PUREE: Place ¼ lb. fresh or thawed frozen blackberries, 2 tablespoons caster (superfine) sugar, 2 tablespoons water, and 2 tablespoons fresh lemon juice in a blender and puree until smooth. Strain before using or storing.

PERIODISTA

CHEZ HENRI
CAMBRIDGE, MASSACHUSETTS

A cocktail that represents New England's contemporary cocktail renaissance, utilizing a classic New England spirit, Medford Rum.

★

GLASSWARE: Coupe
GARNISH: Lime wheel

- 1½ oz. GrandTen Distilling Medford Rum
- ¾ oz. apricot brandy
- ¾ oz. Cointreau
- ½ oz. fresh lime juice

1. Place all of the ingredients in a Boston shaker, fill it two-thirds of the way with ice, and shake for 15 seconds.

2. Strain the cocktail into the coupe, garnish with the lime wheel, and enjoy.

NEW YORK SOUR

Basically an egg white-less whiskey sour with a dash of red wine, this was a popular drink at city speakeasies during Prohibition, where it was used to mask flavors of inferior whiskey.

GLASSWARE: Double rocks glass
GARNISH: Orange wheel, brandied cherry

- **2 oz. Famous Grouse Smoky Black Scotch**
- **¾ oz. Simple Syrup (see recipe)**
- **¾ oz. fresh lemon juice**
- **¼ oz. dry red wine**

1. Place all of the ingredients, except for the wine, in a cocktail shaker, fill it two-thirds of the way with ice, and shake until chilled.

2. Strain the cocktail over ice into the double rocks glass and float the wine on top, pouring it over the back of a spoon.

3. Skewer the orange wheel and brandied cherry on a cocktail pick, garnish the cocktail with it, and enjoy.

SIMPLE SYRUP: Place 1 cup sugar and 1 cup water in a saucepan and bring it to a boil, stirring to dissolve the sugar. Remove the pan from heat and let the syrup cool completely before using or storing.

ALGORITHM OF THE NIGHT

BRAMHALL
PORTLAND, MAINE

Congress Street is Portland's main drag, coursing westward from the East End and its views of Casco Bay, all through downtown, and out to Interstate 295 and the Fore River. As it passes through the sophisticated West End neighborhood, a doorway at Number 769 leads down into a brick-and-stone speakeasy. Lit with candles, subtle sconces, and streaks of light coming through stained-glass windows, it can feel like another time and another place. But it certainly serves a modern array of comfort food and bar snacks, as well as this drink from Bramhall's Jason Rosemeyer. Rosemeyer wanted to combine the flavors of hazelnut and banana, and he found that infusing the noisette-liqueur Frangelico with actual bananas worked better than using a separate banana liqueur, while the allspice bitters toned down the sweetness but kept the complexity.

GLASSWARE: Rocks glass
GARNISH: Dehydrated banana slice

- 2 oz. Ezra Brooks Rye Whiskey
- Dash of Dale DeGroff's Pimento Aromatic Bitters
- 1 oz. Banana-Washed Frangelico (see recipe)

1. Place all of the ingredients in a mixing glass, fill it two-thirds of the way with ice, and stir until chilled.

2. Strain the cocktail over a large ice cube into the rocks glass, garnish with the dehydrated banana slice, and enjoy.

BANANA-WASHED FRANGELICO: Bramhall does a sous-vide water bath for the infusion. For every liter of Frangelico, cut up 3 bananas and throw them into the vacuum bag along with the Frangelico and peels. Set the temperature at 135°F, sous vide for 2 hours, then cool the mixture in an ice bath. Strain and bottle once the mixture is cool.

TURMERIC & TEQUILA

SALT WHARF
CAMDEN, MAINE

On the side of the harbor where Route 1 becomes the main street through the town center is where most of the restaurants and shops reside in this delightfully strollable town. And yet, there is only one restaurant where you can get an ideal view of it, and that's from the other side of the harbor. Its golden vistas pair nicely with a menu of small plates, creative seafood entrees, and even caviar served with house chips. And all of it can be washed down with standards like a Dark & Stormy, or with this funky and refreshing vegetal cocktail from bar manager Meghan Werby.

GLASSWARE: Rocks glass
GARNISH: Dehydrated orange slice, charred;
dehydrated lime slice; pineapple frond

- **Salt, for the rim**
- **Black pepper, freshly cracked, for the rim**
- **2 oz. silver tequila**
- **¼ oz. fresh lemon juice**
- **¼ oz. agave nectar**
- **½ oz. fresh orange juice**
- **1½ oz. Turmeric Juice Blend (see recipe)**

1. Combine salt and pepper in a dish and rim the rocks glass with it.

2. Place the remaining ingredients in a cocktail shaker, fill it two-thirds of the way with ice, and shake until chilled.

3. Strain the cocktail into the rimmed glass and garnish with the dehydrated orange slice, dehydrated lime slice, and pineapple frond.

TURMERIC JUICE BLEND: Use a juicer to combine 1 large carrot, 1 red apple, a 1½-inch-thick slice of freshly skinned pineapple, and 6 to 7 (3- to 4-inch) pieces of fresh turmeric. The juice remains fresh for 5 days, and it can be frozen.

ORCHARD RITA

The Omni's elegant main dining room offers eclectic drinks like an Orchard Rita.

★

GLASSWARE: Collins glass

GARNISH: None

- **Maple sugar, for the rim**
- **Salt, for the rim**
- **1¼ oz. Casamigos Añejo Tequila**
- **¼ oz. fresh lime juice**
- **1 oz. freshly pressed cucumber juice**
- **2 oz. freshly pressed apple juice**

1. Combine maple sugar and salt in a dish and rim the Collins glass with the mixture. Fill the glass with ice.

2. Place the remaining ingredients in a cocktail shaker, fill it two-thirds of the way with ice, and shake until chilled.

3. Strain the cocktail into the rimmed glass and enjoy.

DALE DEGROFF

We likely wouldn't be discussing the American cocktail renaissance if it weren't for the man known as "King Cocktail," who in many ways changed the way we drink. When Dale DeGroff moved to New York in 1969 it was, as he puts it, the end of one era and the beginning of another, with Swing Street giving way to CBGB. "It was a beer and highball, rum and Tab town, then—Chardonnay, a Mimosa or Bloody Mary, maybe you could order a [Sea Breeze] or something made with fake sour mix." However, it was true then as it is now that "adopting a neighborhood bar was to become part of an extended family."

A part-time actor, DeGroff began working in the restaurant industry to make a living before he eventually landed as head bartender at the second revamp of the Rainbow Room in the '80s. Its owner, restaurateur Joe Baum of Restaurant Associates, wanted a classic cocktail menu for the space, which was to have 34 bartenders on staff. He handed DeGroff a copy of *Jerry Thomas' Bartenders Guide* and told him to get busy making drinks. There were simply no other reference materials available, and "the only real cocktail menus in town were at the Bull & Bear, and The Plaza." People began paying attention to the Rainbow Room, which received terrific publicity for its classic concoctions made with fresh juices and quality spirits. DeGroff was at the forefront of this rediscovered ideology for cocktail service—that a good drink is an experience, beginning with the bartender interaction and ending with how the drink tastes and what mood it sets. Things were really changing, he says, "when I went to a bar downtown and saw a Between the Sheets [a Prohibition-era drink] on a cocktail menu."

After the Rainbow Room closed, DeGroff began working in and consulting for other bars in the city (Balthazar, Pravda, Pastis, etc.), mentoring the likes of Audrey Saunders, Julie Reiner, and countless others before finally writing his first book, *The Craft of the Cocktail*, in 2002. ("I guess I was an expert by then," he says.) He is a cofounder of bartender training program Beverage Alcohol Resource (BAR) with David Wondrich, Doug Frost, F. Paul Pacult, Andy Seymour, and Steve Olson, and cofounder of the Museum of the American Cocktail in New Orleans.

FORTH & CLYDE

116 CROWN
NEW HAVEN, CONNECTICUT

Decades ago, Crown Street was once an unsettlingly quiet street once night fell, but in the years since it has exploded as the Elm City's main street for clubs, restaurants, and cocktail meccas like the one residing at 116. Owner John Clark-Ginnetti is such a scholar of cocktail history that he teaches a seminar on cocktail culture and history at nearby Yale University. Here, he shares perhaps his restaurant's most enduring cocktail, which deftly balances bitter, sweet, sour, and heat.

GLASSWARE: Cocktail glass
GARNISH: None

- **Honey, as needed**
- **Red pepper flakes, to taste**
- **1 oz. Hendrick's Gin**
- **1 oz. Maker's Mark Bourbon**
- **1 oz. St-Germain**
- **1 oz. fresh lime juice**

1. Chill the cocktail glass in the freezer.

2. Pour a nickel-sized quantity of honey into a cocktail shaker.

3. Add red pepper flakes and the remaining ingredients and stir until the honey has dissolved.

4. Add as much ice as you can fit into the shaker, and shake for 18 seconds.

5. Strain the cocktail into the chilled cocktail glass and enjoy.

SHIP, CAPTAIN, CREW

BLYTH & BURROWS
PORTLAND, MAINE

By now, it's no secret that Portland is one of the country's premier cities for food and drink—*Bon Appétit* magazine even named it Restaurant City of the Year in 2018—no small feat for a place boasting just 70,000 people. But however hip its current chefs and cocktail gurus may be, they all have a strong sense of their city's long maritime history, thanks to the old brick buildings, narrow cobblestone streets, and working wharfs. The craft cocktail bar Blyth & Burrows is no exception, as it is named after two ship commanders who fought on opposite sides of the War of 1812. At this cozy place with the most current libations, creative director Caleb Landry offers this appropriately named take on a house-smoked Old Fashioned, but one with deeper flavors provided by such subtle flavors as dandelion tea, lemongrass, and spruce tips. If you do not have access to a smoking receptacle, remove the water from the build, and instead stir the cocktail over ice.

GLASSWARE: Rocks glass
GARNISH: Lime slice

- **Tajín, for the rim**
- **1½ oz. Dandelion Bourbon (see recipe)**
- **¼ oz. Smith & Cross Rum**
- **¼ oz. Clement Rhum Premiere Canne**
- **¼ oz. amontillado sherry**
- **¼ oz. Amaro Montenegro**
- **¼ oz. Lemongrass Syrup (see recipe)**
- **¼ oz. water**
- **1 bar spoon Spruce Tip Tincture (see recipe)**

1. Rim the rocks glass with Tajín.

2. Place the remaining ingredients in a smoking receptacle and smoke them.

3. Pour the cocktail into the rimmed glass, garnish with the slice of lime, and enjoy.

DANDELION BOURBON: Steep 2 bags of dandelion tea in 1 liter Wild Turkey 101 Kentucky Straight Bourbon Whiskey for at least 24 hours. Strain before using or storing.

LEMONGRASS SYRUP: Simmer 50 grams chopped lemongrass in 500 ml water, then add the mixture to 1000 grams cane sugar. Stir until the sugar has dissolved and leave the lemongrass in the syrup as it cools. Strain before using or storing.

SPRUCE TIP TINCTURE: Blyth & Burrows forages fresh spruce tips, starting at the end of spring into the beginning of summer. Add 30 grams fresh spruce tips to 1 liter Everclear for the tincture and let it infuse all year, if possible, though infusing for a few days also works.

GIN-GIN MULE

PEGU CLUB
NEW YORK, NEW YORK

This gingery cocktail was created by the massively talented Audrey Saunders at her incredibly influential bar, Pegu Club, as a gateway gin drink for vodka lovers. Not only did it succeed, it inspired many variations around the world. Here is the recipe with her very own specs, including her recipe for Homemade Ginger Beer on the opposite page.

GLASSWARE: Collins glass
GARNISH: Fresh mint, lime wheel, crystallized ginger

- ¾ oz. fresh lime juice
- 1 oz. Simple Syrup (see page 20)
- 1 sprig of fresh mint
- 1 oz. Homemade Ginger Beer
- 1¾ oz. Tanqueray Gin

1. Place the lime juice, syrup, and mint in a cocktail shaker and muddle.

2. Add the ginger beer, gin, and ice and shake vigorously until chilled.

3. Strain over ice into the Collins glass, garnish with the fresh mint, lime wheel, and crystallized ginger, and enjoy.

HOMEMADE GINGER BEER

Says Saunders: "The trick [to the Gin-Gin Mule] is the homemade ginger beer . . . because the store-bought stuff has a peppery (more than gingery) profile—and many times it's insipid." Still, "if you've absolutely got to go there and use the canned stuff, then reduce the Simple Syrup in the drink down to ½ ounce (or less, depending on how sweet the canned stuff is)." This is for a large batch, and should make about 1 gallon.

- **1 gallon water**
- **1 lb. fresh ginger, chopped**
- **4 oz. light brown sugar**
- **2 oz. fresh lime juice**

1. Place the water in a large pot and bring to a boil.

2. Add a cup of the boiling water to a food processor along with the ginger. Blitz until the mixture is almost mulch-like.

3. Place the ginger mixture in the boiling water, turn off the heat, and stir until well combined. Cover the pot and let the mixture steep for 1 hour.

4. Strain the mixture through a chinois, pressing down on the ginger to extract as much liquid and flavor from it as possible. Stir in the brown sugar and lime juice and let the ginger beer cool before carbonating and storing in the refrigerator.

LEAVE IT TO ME (NO. 2)

THE STREET BAR
BOSTON, MASSACHUSETTS

The Newbury Boston may have reopened under that name in 2021, but it's been the premier luxury hotel in Boston since 1927. Back when it was built, it was one of the first Ritz-Carlton hotels in the United States. And it welcomes you to Newbury Street, Boston's deluxe retail thoroughfare where you can find the likes of Chanel, Burberry, Bvlgari, and Armani, as well as many art galleries, salons, and independent boutiques. You can spend a day just being a flaneur and people watching on Newbury Street, then you can finish the day at the hotel with two choices: either have the afternoon tea, which has been served at this location for more than 90 years, or seat yourself at The Street Bar and order up this velvety variation on the classic Clover Club cocktail.

GLASSWARE: Coupe
GARNISH: 3 raspberries

- 2 oz. Grey Goose Vodka
- ¼ oz. Lazzaroni Maraschino liqueur
- ¾ oz. Raspberry Syrup (see recipe)
- ¾ oz. fresh lemon juice
- 1 oz. egg white

1. Place all of the ingredients in a cocktail shaker and dry shake for 15 seconds.

2. Add ice and shake until chilled.

3. Double-strain the cocktail into the coupe, garnish with the raspberries, and enjoy.

RASPBERRY SYRUP: Combine 500 grams raspberries and 500 grams sugar in a deep saucepan, then gently press down the mixture with the back of a fork. Let it macerate for 15 minutes, then add 500 ml water. Set a stove burner to medium heat and bring the mixture to just below a boil. Remove the pan from heat and let the syrup cool for 30 minutes. Strain the syrup through a fine-mesh sieve or cheesecloth before using or storing in the refrigerator.

CROWN SPRITZ

CROWN & ANCHOR
PROVINCETOWN, MASSACHUSETTS

This restaurant-bar-entertainment complex on Provincetown's main drag, Commercial Street, has a slogan that sums it up perfectly: "On a summer's night, the Crown & Anchor can't be missed. In fact, it can't be ignored." Indeed, this building, with its trademark portico and tower, was built to be noticed, as its first incarnation back in the nineteenth century was as an event hall, bowling alley, and saloon. Nowadays, it's a massive epicenter of LGBTQ nightlife and arts, with cabaret drag queens out front welcoming in passersby, who will find inside a boutique hotel, a restaurant, performance venues, a gallery, and six distinctly different bars.

GLASSWARE: Wineglass
GARNISH: Orange twist

- 1½ oz. Aperol
- Prosecco, to top
- Splash of cranberry juice
- 2 fresh mint leaves

1. Fill the wineglass with ice and add the Aperol.
2. Top with Prosecco and add the cranberry juice and fresh mint.
3. Garnish with the orange twist and enjoy.

MANGO CAIPIRINHA

The Dean is downtown Providence's hippest boutique hotel, perhaps made even more decadently hip by the fact that this four-story brick building was built in 1911 as a brothel. But aside from its cool image and sleek rooms, The Dean has preserved many of the old features, such as the original mosaic tile floor and the cage elevator. It also houses The Dean Bar, an evocative, dimly lit craft-cocktail bar, perfect for those chillaxing moments or a romantic tryst.

GLASSWARE: Tiki mug
GARNISH: Fresh cilantro leaf

- **1 fresh cilantro leaf**
- **Pinch of kosher salt**
- **1 oz. Mango Syrup (see recipe)**
- **1½ oz. Tropicana Grog de Cana Rum**
- **½ oz. Pelotón de la Muerte Mezcal**
- **1 oz. fresh lime juice**

1. Place the cilantro leaf and salt in a cocktail shaker. Add the remaining ingredients and 1 ice cube and shake vigorously.

2. Fill the tiki mug with crushed ice and strain the cocktail over it.

3. Garnish with the additional cilantro and enjoy.

MANGO SYRUP: Place 1 cup mango puree and 1 cup Simple Syrup (see page 20) in a mason jar and stir to combine. Use immediately or store in the refrigerator.

HAITIAN DIVORCE

DEAR IRVING
NEW YORK, NEW YORK

This sherry-focused cocktail by Tom Richter now resides at Dear Irving, but was created at The Beagle and is replicated at many bars across the city.

★

GLASSWARE: Double rocks glass
GARNISH: Orange twist, lime twist

- 1½ oz. Rhum Barbancourt 5 Star Rum
- ¾ oz. Del Maguey Vida Mezcal
- ½ oz. Pedro Ximénez sherry
- 2 dashes of Angostura Bitters

1. Place all of the ingredients in the rocks glass, add large ice cubes, and stir until chilled.

2. Garnish with the orange twist and lime twist and enjoy.

MARCELINO'S BOUTIQUE BAR

The Omni Providence Hotel towers above the city with glorious views of the state capitol building in one direction; in the other direction, guests can see the Providence River widen out into Narragansett Bay. But on the ground, the doors on the windswept corner of Exchange and Fountain Streets lead you into an otherworldly experience at Marcelino's Boutique Bar. With an ideal balance of opulent lights, evocative shadows, and atmospheric music, you can wander through a space that feels larger than it is as you choose whether to sit at the bar, at a low-top table, or even in an intimate speakeasy room. And then there are the cocktails. Simply named after pairs of flavors—like Pineapple | Vetiver (see page 45)—these carefully handcrafted drinks themselves are each an intriguing bounty, delicious but complex, presented with naturalistic garnishes clipped to the side of the glass. It's a getaway where you will want to spend hours, and it's a vision whose origins lie thousands of miles away in the Middle East.

Marcelino Abou Ali grew up in Batroun, Lebanon, a seaside city that is one of the oldest inhabited municipalities in the world. His grandparents were farmers, growing oranges, peaches, tomatoes, and any number of vegetables, and being around them inspires him to this day. "When my grandmother wanted to make tomato paste, I could always smell her smoking the tomatoes. We grew up like other people there, creating and crafting everything, since back then you had to have a field in order to eat. Whatever you need, you just have to make yourself."

By the time he was a teenager, Marcelino was sleeping on the first floor of his grandmother's house so he could sneak out at night and work in the clubs in the resort town of Jounieh, a half hour's drive down the coast. In 2007, at a beach bar there, Marcelino's manager introduced him to another young nightlife upstart named Refaat Ghostine, and their friendship and careers have been linked together since then. Over the next few years, the two young men worked their way up from being barbacks in Jounieh to working in Beirut's premier club, Buddha Bar. Marcelino eventually would travel around the region doing star turns working as a "flair bartender," delivering drinks with dazzling feats of bottle-tossing acrobatics, and investing in new bars and clubs as a partner. Meanwhile, in 2014, Refaat became head bartender at Beirut's Central Station Boutique Bar, where he gained renown for his creative use of a rotary evaporator for vacuum distilling and a centrifuge for separating and clarifying ingredients—Central Station was a regular on the World's 50 Best Bars annual list, and Refaat himself was named World Class Country Winner by Diageo in 2015.

Nevertheless, the United States beckoned when Marcelino's family moved to New England in 2015 so that his younger brother Pascal could go to school there, and Marcelino found himself in Rhode Island starting his career over again, working tirelessly anywhere he could, whether at a gas station or finally managing a place in Federal Hill, Providence's Little Italy. And it was there that he made his name with customers for his professional service as a host, and where his dream of opening his own place came to fruition, thanks to one of his regulars, a dentist named Basel Badawi. "I gave him very good service; he liked my attitude and discipline and asked me what's my goal," Marcelino says. "I said I'm working toward it; I want to open an experience, I want to build a brand. But to start, I need a space. And he said, 'Why don't we do this thing together?'" And so the two men became partners, and then in 2018 when they signed for the space on the ground floor of the Omni, they became co-owners of Marcelino's Boutique Bar.

Marcelino immediately obsessed about the challenging, warren-like space, carefully choosing every lighting fixture, every decoration in every nook, every music speaker in every room. With his experience, he knew he could do a good job with creating a cocktail program, but he felt that if he did his best with the interior design, why not get the best bartender he knew? Refaat was working in Dubai at the time, and when Marcelino asked him to come to his adopted home state to create a bar, Refaat asked what island he was talking about. "I said, 'Rhode Island,'" Marcelino laughs. "He thought it was actually an island! But then he came here and inspired people. He's the cream on top of the cake."

The bar opened in 2020, with the cocktail menu created by Refaat, using the fundamental flavors and ingredients of the Middle East that they grew up eating and drinking, and applying the advanced techniques that he perfected back home. And it was also Refaat's idea to keep the cocktail names bluntly simple, both to do something different, but also to give customers a clear idea of what their drink will taste like. "I do believe in getting straight to the point," Marcelino says. "Not everybody is a bartender, so you can't expect people to just understand what you're tasting. So we made it in a way to get to people's minds and hearts with the title, so they can understand more and help them make a better choice."

Now with his old friend bringing his artistry to his adopted hometown and his brother Pascal doing the accounting and purchasing, Marcelino has seen his aspirations come full circle. "Even when I was a kid in school, I dreamed about coming to America even if I didn't know much about it," he says. "And now this place feels like home. It was a long way from 2015 to opening in 2020, but if it wasn't challenging, it would have been boring."

PINEAPPLE | VETIVER

MARCELINO'S BOUTIQUE BAR
PROVIDENCE, RHODE ISLAND

Refaat Ghostine sums up this drink as "a cocktail creation that infuses two classic drinks, the Piña Colada and the Vesper Martini, with a modern twist, creating a Vesper Colada." Ingredients like pineapple, coconut, and Cocchi Americano are certainly familiar, but what puts the drink on a different level is the grassy vetiver, which adds an earthy and woody flavor, creating a more exotic taste profile. Due to the precision required, the measurements are given in metric.

GLASSWARE: Nick & Nora glass
GARNISH: Dehydrated pineapple chunk

- **80 ml Blended Infusion** (see recipe)
- **Dash of orange bitters**
- **4 ml 20 Percent Citric Acid Solution (see recipe)**
- **4 ml Simple Syrup** (see page 20)
- **4 drops of coconut oil**

1. Place all of the ingredients, except the coconut oil, in a mixing glass, fill it two-thirds of the way with ice, and stir until chilled.

2. Strain the cocktail into the Nick & Nora glass and top with the coconut oil.

3. Garnish with the dehydrated pineapple chunk and enjoy.

BLENDED INFUSION: Combine 40 ml gin, 20 ml vodka, and 20 ml Cocchi Americano and add fresh pineapple and dried vetiver to taste. Let the mixture steep until the taste is to your liking and strain before using or storing.

20 PERCENT CITRIC ACID SOLUTION: Place 80 ml water and 20 grams citric acid in a mason jar and stir until the citric acid has dissolved. Use as desired.

BLOOD, LUST & DIAMONDS

CREATED BY BRYAN TEOH
NEW YORK, NEW YORK

According to the cocktail's creator, Bryan Teoh, the name is inspired by "a quote by Jacobean dramatist John Webster, 'Whether we fall by ambition, blood, or lust, Like diamonds, we are cut with our own dust.'"

GLASSWARE: Coupe
GARNISH: Maraschino cherry

- 2 oz. rye whiskey
- ¾ oz. Bonal Gentiane Quina
- ½ oz. Cognac
- Dash of Angostura Bitters
- Dash of Peychaud's Bitters
- Dash of Amaretto

1. Place all of the ingredients in a mixing glass, fill it two-thirds of the way with ice, and stir until chilled.

2. Strain the cocktail into the coupe, garnish with the maraschino cherry, and enjoy.

FEAR FACTOR

PARLA
BOSTON, MASSACHUSETTS

Surrounded by Italian restaurants on the main drag of Boston's North End, Parla is a Mediterranean restaurant whose interior and cuisine manage a glowing balance between rustic charm and urban cool. And so it is with their cocktails. As general manager Patrick Panageas explains, he was inspired by his Greek and Portuguese heritage to create this "exploration of olive oil as it pertains to the cocktail world."

GLASSWARE: Coupe
GARNISH: Amargo Chuncho Bitters, furikake, dried crickets

- 1½ oz. Del Maguey Crema de Mezcal

- ½ oz. Licor 43

- ½ oz. fresh lemon juice

- ¼ oz. extra-virgin olive oil

- ¼ oz. Honey Syrup (see page 73)

- ¼ oz. Roasted Beet Shrub (see recipe on page 49)

- 1 egg white

1. Chill the coupe in the freezer.

2. Place all of the ingredients in a cocktail shaker and dry shake for 15 seconds.

3. Add ice and shake until chilled.

4. Double-strain the cocktail into the chilled coupe, garnish with bitters, furikake, and dried crickets, and enjoy.

ROASTED BEET SHRUB: Preheat the oven to 375°F. Put 4 whole beets in a deep baking pan, fill one-third of the pan with cold water, and cover it with aluminum foil. Place the pan in the oven and bake for 35 minutes. Remove the pan from the oven and remove the aluminum foil. After allowing the beets to cool, peel them and chop them into 1-inch cubes (be sure to wear gloves to avoid staining your hands). Place the beets in a bowl and add enough sugar to coat every surface of the beets. Place the beets in the refrigerator and chill for 6 to 8 hours. Strain through a fine-mesh sieve and add white distilled vinegar at a 2:1 ratio of yielded sugar juice to vinegar. Use immediately or store in the refrigerator for up to 3 weeks.

TIA MIA

LEYENDA
NEW YORK, NEW YORK

Adding just a little smoke to the Mai Tai provides a far more thoughtful experience.

GLASSWARE: Rocks glass
GARNISH: Fresh mint, lime wheel, edible orchid blossom

- 1 oz. mezcal
- 1 oz. aged Jamaican rum
- ¾ oz. fresh lime juice
- ½ oz. Orgeat (see recipe)
- ½ oz. Pierre Ferrand Dry Curaçao

1. Place all of the ingredients in a cocktail shaker, fill it two-thirds of the way with ice, and shake until chilled.
2. Fill the rocks glass with crushed ice and strain the cocktail over it.
3. Garnish with the fresh mint, lime wheel, and edible orchid and enjoy.

ORGEAT: Preheat the oven to 400°F. Place 2 cups almonds on a baking sheet, place them in the oven, and toast until they are fragrant, about 5 minutes. Remove the almonds from the oven and let them cool completely. Place the almonds in a food processor and pulse until they are a coarse meal. Set the almonds aside. Place 1 cup Demerara Syrup (see page 63) in a saucepan and warm it over medium heat. Add the almond meal, remove the pan from heat, and let the mixture steep for 6 hours. Strain the mixture through cheesecloth and discard the solids. Stir in 1 teaspoon orange blossom water and 2 oz. vodka and use immediately or store in the refrigerator.

NEON GOD

The Archives is such a vibrant, unique bar that one location can't contain it. There is one Archives in the bustling college town of Burlington, and another in nearby Winooski, which has recently become Vermont's latest hot spot for nightlife. Featuring local craft beers from a state that has some of the most lauded microbreweries in the country, The Archives also has classic and new cocktails, as well as vintage arcade games. If the Neon God sounds like a video game...well, the name for this brightly colored Daiquiri actually comes from the Simon & Garfunkel song "The Sound of Silence." Beverage director Sean McKenzie explains that he likes the evocative line in the song, which provided a cool image for this spirit-forward, aromatic cocktail that's anchored by a split base of full-flavored higher-proof rums.

GLASSWARE: Double rocks glass
GARNISH: None

- 1½ oz. Rhum J.M Agricole Blanc (100 proof)
- 1 oz. pineapple juice
- ½ oz. fresh lime juice
- ½ oz. Vanilla Syrup (see page 371)
- ¼ oz. Smith & Cross Rum
- ¼ oz. Amaro Montenegro

1. Chill the double rocks glass in the freezer.

2. Place all of the ingredients in a cocktail shaker, fill it two-thirds of the way with ice, and shake until chilled.

3. Double-strain the cocktail into the chilled glass and enjoy.

OAXACA OLD FASHIONED

DEATH & CO
NEW YORK, NEW YORK

Created by agave spirits evangelist Phil Ward at the infamous Death & Co, this is the cocktail that got the cocktail world excited about mezcal. Don't be afraid to experiment with the type of bitters employed in this one—in an evolved version Ward went with Bittermens Xocolatl Mole Bitters—or to go all in on a mezcal-only version.

GLASSWARE: Rocks glass

GARNISH: Strip of orange peel

- 1½ oz. reposado tequila
- ½ oz. mezcal
- 2 dashes of Angostura Bitters
- 1 bar spoon agave nectar

1. Place a large ice cube in the rocks glass. Add all of the ingredients and stir until chilled.

2. Hold the strip of orange peel about 2 inches above a lit match for a couple of seconds. Twist and squeeze the peel over the lit match, while holding it above the cocktail and taking care to avoid the flames.

3. Rub the torched peel around the rim of the glass, drop it into the drink, and enjoy.

JASMINE HORCHATA: Add 16 cups warm water and 4 cups jasmine rice to a Cambro container. In a cold-brew bag, add the peels of 4 oranges and 8 bags of sencha green tea. Place the cold-brew bag in the Cambro container and let the mixtures sit overnight. Remove the cold-brew bag and then stir the rice and water together until the rice has swollen to the size of BB pellets. Do not overblend. Strain the mixture through a fine-mesh sieve, place it in a saucepan, and then warm it to 140°F. Add 2,250 grams Domino Sugar and 100 grams lactic acid and stir until they have dissolved. Let the horchata cool completely before using or storing.

SPIRITED AWAY

BLYTH & BURROWS
PORTLAND, MAINE

Caleb Landry, the creative director at Blyth & Burrows, says that this drink immediately became a huge hit when they introduced it in spring 2019. It's light and floral, and easy for the home bartender to assemble, except for making the horchata out of jasmine rice. But Landry points out that the lactic acid powder is easy to find online or in brewery supply stores, and the extra effort is worth the result. "The batch can be scaled down pretty easily—I'd divide it by four," Landry says. "But it never hurts to have a little extra in the fridge, because it drinks great by itself or with some soda if you're looking for a fun non-alcoholic option."

GLASSWARE: Collins glass
GARNISH: Cherry blossom

- 2 oz. soda water
- 1½ oz. shochu
- 2 oz. Jasmine Horchata (see recipe)
- ½ oz. Haku Vodka

1. Place the soda water in the Collins glass to encourage the "fluffing" of the horchata.

2. Place the remaining ingredients in a cocktail shaker, add 1 ice cube, and shake vigorously.

3. Strain the mixture over the soda water, garnish with the cherry blossom, and enjoy.

DAVID WONDRICH

Writer and historian David Wondrich has become one of the go-to consultants when you want to party like it's 1899. Need to re-create a lost spirit? Find out who was behind the stick at the long-gone City Hotel? Learn the proper measurements for an old recipe that vaguely recommends using a "pony" of an ingredient? Call Dave.

Wondrich says his career began through the "law of unintended consequences."

Really, all he and his wife wanted was to find a good drink. "We liked our bars, but we just wanted them to make better cocktails." It wasn't easy. One had to know where they were, and which bar made what drink well. After a day at The Met, for example, go to Bemelmans for the Stinger or find the good bartender at Joe Allen in the theater district, or visit Del Pedro at Grange Hall. Per Wondrich, it was a matter of, "'Hey! The guy here can make a Sidecar! This guy over here makes a Manhattan!' It's not as though we were dying of thirst. Everyone could make a decent Martini. Although even elegant bars would make shit drinks."

Part of the problem is what Wondrich refers to as the "dumbing down" of drinks. Spirits came with terrible recipe cards and venues would make those drinks as an incentive to get better deals on the products. "Drinks like the Fuzzy Navel were invented in a corporate boardroom."

Cut to the late 1990s and the rise of the internet. Wondrich found himself aligning with like-minded "cocktail geeks" like Robert Hess, who had the DrinkBoy cocktail site—a favorite forum for posting cocktail findings that attracted readers like Audrey Saunders and Ted Haigh. At the time, Wondrich was an English professor and music writer for *Esquire*.

The writing pivoted toward cocktails, and because it was way more fun, cocktail writing took over.

The rest is history. Lots of history. His books include *Imbibe!* and *Punch*, and he's written countless columns for *Esquire*, *Eater*, and *Imbibe*, among many other publications. He has also consulted on quite a few spirits projects, including Pierre Ferrand Dry Curaçao and Plantation's O.F.T.D. Rum.

NAKED & FAMOUS

DEATH & CO
NEW YORK, NEW YORK

The salmon pink color is a bit deceptive, as the drink is smoky thanks to the mezcal and bittersweet thanks to the Aperol. This mash-up of the Last Word and the Paper Plane was another massive hit from the folks at New York's Death & Co.

★

GLASSWARE: Coupe
GARNISH: None

- ¾ oz. mezcal
- ¾ oz. Yellow Chartreuse
- ¾ oz. Aperol
- ¾ oz. fresh lime juice

1. Chill the coupe in the freezer.

2. Place all of the ingredients in a cocktail shaker, fill it two-thirds of the way with ice, and shake until chilled.

3. Strain into the chilled coupe and enjoy.

FLIRTBIRD

ANGEL'S SHARE
NEW YORK, NEW YORK

This take on the Jungle Bird, a tiki classic, makes artful use of popular Japanese ingredients.

★

GLASSWARE: Clay cup
GARNISH: Shiso leaf

- Plum powder, for the rim
- 1 fresh shiso leaf
- 1½ oz. shochu
- 1 oz. fresh yuzu juice
- ½ oz. agave nectar

1. Wet the rim of the cup and coat it with the plum powder.

2. Tear the shiso leaf in half and add it to a cocktail shaker along with the remaining ingredients. Fill the shaker two-thirds of the way with ice and shake vigorously until chilled.

3. Strain the cocktail over a large ice cube into the cup, garnish with the additional shiso leaf, and enjoy.

DAUPHIN

LE BOUDOIR
BROOKLYN, NEW YORK

Bartender Franky Marshall, a Clover Club alum, has a way with outside-the-box ingredients, as this inventive serve shows.

GLASSWARE: Collins glass
GARNISH: Cacao nibs, star anise pod

- 1½ oz. Goslings Black Seal Rum
- 2 dashes of Miracle Mile Bitters Co. Chocolate Chili Bitters
- ½ oz. Demerara Syrup (see recipe)
- ½ oz. Ancho Reyes
- 1 oz. absinthe
- 1¼ oz. toasted coconut almond milk

1. Place the Collins glass in a bowl and build the cocktail in the glass, adding the ingredients in the order they are listed.

2. Fill the bowl and the glass with pebble ice and stir the cocktail until it is chilled and combined.

3. Garnish with the cacao nibs and star anise and enjoy.

DEMERARA SYRUP: Place 1 cup water in a saucepan and bring it to a boil. Add ½ cup demerara sugar and 1½ cups sugar and stir until they have dissolved. Remove the pan from heat and let the syrup cool completely before using or storing.

JOY DIVISION

DEATH & CO
NEW YORK, NEW YORK

Here's a crowd favorite created by Phil Ward that is still in high demand—at Death & Co, and bars across the world.

★

GLASSWARE: Coupe
GARNISH: Lemon twist

- 2 oz. Beefeater Gin
- 1 oz. Dolin Blanc
- ½ oz. Cointreau

- 3 dashes of Vieux Pontarlier Absinthe

1. Place all of the ingredients in a mixing glass, fill it two-thirds of the way with ice, and stir until chilled.

2. Strain the cocktail into the coupe, garnish with the lemon twist, and enjoy.

MACE

An elegant serve courtesy of the team at New York's Mace, Nico de Soto and Greg Boehm.

★

GLASSWARE: Coupe
GARNISH: Spritz of mace tincture

- 1 oz. Linie Aquavit
- 1 oz. Aperol
- ½ oz. fresh orange juice
- ½ oz. freshly pressed beet juice
- ¾ oz. syrup from a can of Lucia young coconut

1. Place all of the ingredients in a cocktail shaker, fill it two-thirds of the way with ice, and shake vigorously until chilled.

2. Double-strain the cocktail into the coupe, spritz it with the mace tincture, and enjoy.

Q & A WITH GREG BOEHM

Greg Boehm is the owner of Cocktail Kingdom and several acclaimed New York City bars, such as Mace. He's had his finger on the pulse of contemporary cocktail culture for more than two decades, and his deep appreciation for the history of cocktails is a big part of the reason why.

Can you tell us a bit about yourself and how you got into the industry?

Sterling, my family's publishing company, published *Classic Cocktails* by Salvatore Calabrese in 1997. At that time I would be in London fairly often, and I spent many of those nights at The Library Bar, where Salvatore's team would make amazing cocktails. I was hooked, and I started collecting antique cocktail books as my interest in cocktails grew. A couple years later I started importing high-quality barware, and finally started designing and manufacturing barware.

What can you tell us about the creation of Cocktail Kingdom?

Cocktail Kingdom started when I published very accurate facsimile reproductions of some of the most important cocktail books from the 1800s and early 1900s. As I came to know many great bartenders, I was asked to import barware from Japan and Germany, which I did. After talking with many of the top bartenders, I realized there was an opportunity to design and sell barware both based on antiques and more modern styles. Today, Cocktail Kingdom sells barware and glassware to more than 60 countries.

What are the themes of your bars?

Boilermaker is my oldest bar. I wanted to create a place that was more of a "local" that could also make great cocktails. It is the kind of bar that gets better with age. I was actually happy when the banquettes started to get beat up a little. Mace was the next bar that I opened. Nico de Soto was one of my absolute favorite bartenders. The cocktails he made were so good. So he and I decided to open a small bar with spice-focused cocktails. Since Nico and I travel so extensively, and spices are truly international, it was a good fit. The walls are decorated with jars of spices that I carried back from places like Madagascar and India.

What do you and your team look for when starting a new bar?

I just go with gut instinct when deciding to open a new bar. I do not even put together a business plan. It is all about team building for me. Of course, finding the right space for the right price is important too.

THE ESCAPE

THE RUM HOUSE
NEW YORK, NEW YORK

Sprucing up a Piña Colada with a bit of sweet vermouth adds an irresistible depth.

★

GLASSWARE: Brandy snifter
GARNISH: Pineapple chunk, maraschino cherry

- 2 oz. El Dorado Single Barrel Demerara Rum
- 1 oz. pineapple juice
- 1 oz. cream of coconut
- ¾ oz. sweet vermouth

1. Place the rum, pineapple juice, and cream of coconut in a cocktail shaker, fill it two-thirds of the way with ice, and shake until chilled.

2. Fill the brandy snifter with crushed ice and strain the cocktail over it.

3. Float the vermouth on top of the cocktail, pouring it over the back of a bar spoon.

4. Garnish with the pineapple chunk and maraschino cherry and enjoy.

LAWYERS, GUNS & MONEY

SLOWLY SHIRLEY
NEW YORK, NEW YORK

Slowly Shirley, where the atmosphere is akin to an old-school Hollywood nightclub, is "more for people who pay attention to a drink the same way they pay attention to a good dish when eating out," says founder Jim Kearns. Kearns's cocktails have found admirers all across New York, including from some of the cocktail scene's brightest lights.

GLASSWARE: Rocks glass
GARNISH: Cocoa powder, chili powder, orange twist

- 1½ oz. Cotes du Rhone
- ½ oz. ruby Port
- ½ oz. Pedro Ximénez sherry
- ½ oz. Rhum Barbancourt 5 Star Rum
- 2 dashes of Amargo Chuncho Bitters
- 2 dashes of Bittermens Hellfire Habanero Shrub
- ¼ oz. crème de cacao

1. Place all of the ingredients in a cocktail shaker, fill it two-thirds of the way with ice, and shake vigorously until chilled.
2. Fill the rocks glass with pebble ice and strain the cocktail over it.
3. Garnish the cocktail with cocoa powder, chili powder, and the orange twist and enjoy.

GINS & ROSES

THE WREN
NEW YORK, NEW YORK

From The Wren co-owner Krissy Harris: "I'm constantly challenging myself to use ingredients that I find difficult to work with. In this case, rose. I had never enjoyed rose water, but after tasting Giffard Black Rose Liqueur, I was inspired to create a cocktail that could celebrate the rose but not be dominated by it. Martin Miller's Gin has a softness to it while still staying true to the London Dry style, so I often turn to it when making cocktails. Cocchi Rosa Americano is a wonderful aperitif wine that is both aromatic and slightly bitter from the quinine. These three ingredients, combined with a splash of freshly squeezed lemon juice, create a well-balanced, refreshingly floral cocktail."

GLASSWARE: Rocks glass

GARNISH: Dried rosebuds

- 1 oz. Martin Miller's Gin
- 1 oz. Cocchi Rosa Americano
- ½ oz. fresh lemon juice
- ½ oz. Giffard Black Rose Liqueur
- ¼ oz. Honey Syrup (see recipe)

1. Place all of the ingredients in a cocktail shaker, fill it two-thirds of the way with ice, and shake until chilled.

2. Strain over ice into the rocks glass, garnish with the dried rosebuds, and enjoy.

HONEY SYRUP: Place 1½ cups water in a saucepan and bring it to a boil. Add 1½ cups honey and cook until it is just runny. Remove the pan from heat and let the syrup cool before using or storing in the refrigerator.

THIRD PLAYER

THE BONNIE
ASTORIA, NEW YORK

A cocktail that runs in a number of directions, yet is still comforting and accessible, thanks to the sense of campfire elicited by the smoke and warming spices.

GLASSWARE: Rocks glass
GARNISH: Crushed cinnamon sticks

- ¾ oz. mezcal
- ½ oz. cachaça
- ½ oz. Toasted Black Cardamom & Cinnamon Maple Syrup (see recipe)
- ½ oz. fresh lime juice
- ¼ oz. pisco
- ¼ oz. apricot liqueur
- ¼ oz. Ancho Reyes
- ½ oz. Orgeat (see page 50)
- ¼ oz. falernum
- 2 dashes of Bittermens Xocolatl Mole Bitters
- Pinch of salt

1. Place all of the ingredients in a cocktail shaker, fill it two-thirds of the way with ice, and shake until chilled.
2. Fill the rocks glass with crushed ice and strain the cocktail over it.
3. Garnish with crushed cinnamon sticks and enjoy.

TOASTED BLACK CARDAMOM & CINNAMON MAPLE SYRUP: Place 2 cinnamon sticks and 3 black cardamom pods in a skillet and toast over medium heat until fragrant, shaking the pan frequently. Remove the aromatics from the pan and set them aside. Place 1 cup maple syrup and ½ cup water in a saucepan and bring to a simmer. Add the toasted spices and simmer for 5 minutes. Remove the pan from heat and let the mixture cool for 1 hour. Strain before using or storing.

LOST IN TRANSLATION

DANIEL
NEW YORK, NEW YORK

Perhaps it is only a trick of the mind, but the green hue lent by the matcha powder seems to make the grassy nature of cachaça and the green apple notes in shochu all the more powerful.

GLASSWARE: Clay bowl
GARNISH: Dusting of matcha powder

- 1 oz. cachaça
- 1 oz. shochu
- ½ oz. fresh lime juice
- ¾ oz. Simple Syrup (see page 20)
- ¼ teaspoon matcha powder
- ¾ oz. egg white

1. Place all of the ingredients in a cocktail shaker and dry shake for 10 seconds.

2. Add ice and shake until chilled.

3. Double-strain the cocktail into the clay bowl, top with the dusting of matcha powder, and enjoy.

MID-ATLANTIC

Pineapple & Cardamom Milk Punch

Elevated Brilliance ★ Omar's Fizz

Teatime Across the Pond

Sun Breaking Through the Fog

El Nopal ★ Gin Grin

Madame Lee ★ Oaxacan Bottlerocket

Gotta Roll ★ A Stone's Throw

4 Grapes ★ Absinthe Rickey

Prelude to a Kiss

Once you've gotten your fill of the elegant takes on tradition that hold sway in bars in the Northeast, it's time for us to pack up and head down 95 to Washington, D.C., the country's capital.

And again, we find that the signal we receive from afar is actually noise when we get up close. For the image we may have in our heads about D.C.—lobbyists and other political players sitting around soulless steak houses, smirking at the stupidity of the little people over an endless series of vodka Martinis—is continually overturned and upset during our tour of the town's bars. At ground level, The District is a veritable garden of delights for the cocktail connoisseur, with Michelin-starred restaurants fashioning clarified punches, a team of geniuses who have made the unfamiliar elements of Afghani cuisine accessible to a global audience, a take on tiki that no doubt brings some much needed levity to the town, an eye-catching twist on the Daiquiri that is intriguingly built around Pimm's, and many more.

PINEAPPLE & CARDAMOM MILK PUNCH

THE IMPERIAL
WASHINGTON, D.C.

Michelin-honored The Imperial is the sister bar to Jack Rose, and it has a focus on cocktails that use creative and unique techniques, as in this punch, which tricks the eye by delivering so many flavors in a crystal-clear cocktail.

GLASSWARE: Rocks glass

GARNISH: Lemon twist

- 10 cardamom pods
- Peels of 2 lemons
- Peels of 2 oranges
- 29 oz. pisco
- 3 oz. crème de cacao
- 8 oz. fresh lemon juice
- 8 oz. fresh pineapple juice
- 15 oz. Simple Syrup (see page 20)
- 8 oz. milk

1. Crack the cardamom pods to release their oils. Combine the pods, fruit peels, and pisco in a vacuum bag and seal it.

2. Sous vide the mixture at 135°F for 2 hours. Strain the mixture and set it aside. If you do not have a sous vide machine, you can place the mixture in a large mason jar and let it sit for about a week at room temperature, agitating it once a day. Combine the cardamom-pisco mixture, crème de cacao, lemon and pineapple juice, and Simple Syrup in a large glass vessel.

3. Slowly add the milk and give it a good stir to incorporate. Let the mixture curdle and then set it in the refrigerator overnight.

4. Set up a coffee filter to strain the mixture into your desired container for service. Strain the punch, 3 oz. at a time, into a mixing glass filled with ice, and stir until the punch is chilled and diluted.

5. To serve, pour the punch over a large ice cube into the rocks glass, garnish with the lemon twist, and enjoy.

RECYCLED ESPRESSO BEANS: Place 1 melted chocolate bar and 1½ teaspoons Cacao Nib & Espresso Solids in a mixing bowl and stir to combine. Pour the mixture into a silicone coffee bean mold. If this mold is not available, the mixture can also be spread on a parchment-lined baking sheet to make a kind of bark. Place the beans in the freezer until set, about 10 minutes. Remove the beans from the mold and use immediately or store in the refrigerator.

ELEVATED BRILLIANCE

THE LEFT BANK RESTAURANT & BAR
YORK, PENNSYLVANIA

Every single element here is used to the fullest, a reality that is reinforced with the recycled garnish.

★

GLASSWARE: Coupe
GARNISH: 3 Recycled Espresso Beans (see recipe)

- ¼ oz. fresh lemon juice
- ¼ oz. Toasted Cacao Nib & Espresso Brew (see recipe)
- ½ oz. Cardamom & Honey Syrup (see recipe)
- 1½ oz. Paul John Brilliance Whisky

1. Chill the coupe in the freezer.
2. Place all of the ingredients in a cocktail shaker, fill it two-thirds of the way with ice, and shake until chilled.
3. Strain into the chilled coupe, garnish with the Recycled Espresso Beans, and enjoy.

TOASTED CACAO NIB & ESPRESSO BREW: Place ½ teaspoon cacao nibs in a dry skillet and toast over medium heat, shaking the pan frequently, until they start to sweat and become extremely fragrant, about 10 minutes. Place the cacao nibs in a mason jar, add ½ teaspoon finely ground espresso and 2 tablespoons luke-warm water, and let the mixture steep overnight. Strain the mixture through a fine-mesh sieve before using or storing in the refrigerator. Reserve the solids for use in the Recycled Espresso Beans.

CARDAMOM & HONEY SYRUP: Place ½ cup wildflower honey, ¼ cup water, and ½ teaspoon ground cardamom in a saucepan and bring to a simmer over medium-low heat, stirring until the honey has emulsified. Remove the pan from heat and let the syrup cool. Strain the syrup through a fine-mesh sieve before using or storing in the refrigerator.

OMAR'S FIZZ

LAPIS
WASHINGTON, D.C.

The immigrant-owned Lapis translates traditional Afghan flavors into modern takes on food and drink. From the bar, guests can expect cocktails made with the country's signature ingredients. Omar's Fizz is inspired by firnee, a custard dessert made with cardamom, pistachio, rose water, and saffron.

GLASSWARE: Collins glass
GARNISH: Shiso leaves

- 1½ oz. Saffron-Infused Singani (see recipe)
- 1 oz. Vanilla Syrup (see page 371)
- 1 oz. fresh lemon juice
- 1 oz. heavy cream
- 3 dashes of cardamom bitters
- 1 egg white
- Splash of club soda, to top

1. Place all of the ingredients, except for the club soda, in a cocktail shaker and dry shake for 10 seconds.

2. Add ice and shake until chilled. Let the cocktail rest for 30 seconds.

3. Strain over ice into the Collins glass and top with the club soda.

4. Garnish with shiso leaves and enjoy.

SAFFRON-INFUSED SINGANI: Place 2 pinches of saffron threads and a 750 ml bottle of Singani 63 in a large mason jar and let the mixture steep overnight. Strain before using or storing.

TEATIME ACROSS THE POND

THE LEFT BANK RESTAURANT & BAR
YORK, PENNSYLVANIA

If you're looking to make teatime a bit more fun, this elegant serve is a great option.

★

GLASSWARE: Teacup
GARNISH: Fresh mint

- **2½ oz. Green Tea–Infused Gin (see recipe)**
- **¼ oz. Yellow Chartreuse**
- **½ oz. Raspberry Syrup (see page 35)**

1. Chill the teacup in the freezer.

2. Place all of the ingredients in a cocktail shaker, fill it two-thirds of the way with ice, and shake until chilled.

3. Strain the cocktail into the chilled teacup, garnish with fresh mint, and enjoy.

GREEN TEA–INFUSED GIN: Place ½ cup Aviation Gin and 1 bag of organic green tea in a mason jar and let the mixture steep until the flavor is bright, about 25 minutes. Remove the tea bag and use immediately or store.

SUN BREAKING THROUGH THE FOG

BRESCA
WASHINGTON, D.C.

At Bresca, chef Ryan Ratino serves up elevated French-inspired food that's both modern and exciting. The bar program carries on that ethos, pulling techniques from across the history of cocktails. Bar director Will Patton uses Monet's famous impressionist painting as a muse for a rum drink with tikiesque vibes for this cocktail.

GLASSWARE: Collins glass
GARNISH: Yellow viola blossom

- ¾ oz. Ten to One Caribbean Dark Rum
- ¾ oz. Fonseca 10-Year Tawny Port
- ¾ oz. Amaro Montenegro
- ¾ oz. fresh lime juice
- ¾ oz. Pineapple Syrup (see recipe)

1. Place all of the ingredients in a cocktail shaker, fill it two-thirds of the way with ice, and shake until chilled.
2. Fill the Collins glass with crushed ice and strain the cocktail over it.
3. Garnish with the yellow viola blossom and enjoy.

PINEAPPLE SYRUP: Combine equal parts pineapple juice and sugar in a blender and blend on high for 2 minutes. Let the syrup settle, then transfer it to a container and chill in the refrigerator until ready to use.

EL NOPAL

MAÏZ64
WASHINGTON, D.C.

Wanting a refreshing new addition to the cocktail menu, Roberto Andraca borrowed flavors from a salad that Maïz64 head chef Alam Méndez Florian prepared, which featured the bright, green notes of fennel and cactus.

★

GLASSWARE: Coupe
GARNISH: 2 spritzes of mezcal

- 1 oz. Mexican rum
- ¾ oz. Fennel & Cactus Syrup (see recipe)
- ¾ oz. fresh lemon juice
- ½ oz. Ancho Reyes Verde

1. Place all of the ingredients in a cocktail shaker, fill it two-thirds of the way with ice, and shake until chilled.

2. Strain the cocktail into the coupe, spritz with the mezcal, and enjoy.

FENNEL & CACTUS SYRUP: Add 500 ml Simple Syrup (see page 20), 60 grams cleaned, chopped cactus, and 50 grams fennel stems with the fronds to a blender and blend until smooth. Strain before using or storing in the refrigerator.

GIN GRIN

OKPB
WASHINGTON, D.C.

This easy drinking mix of Aperol, lemon juice, and mint is a simple and refreshing drink that's sure to brighten any occasion.

GLASSWARE: Rocks glass
GARNISH: Fresh mint

- ½ lemon
- 1½ oz. gin
- ½ oz. Aperol
- ¾ oz. Simple Syrup (see page 20)
- 2 dashes of Angostura Bitters
- 5 to 6 fresh mint leaves

1. Place the lemon in a cocktail shaker and muddle it.
2. Add ice and the remaining ingredients and shake short and vigorously.
3. Strain the cocktail into the rocks glass and top with cracked ice.
4. Garnish with fresh mint and enjoy.

MADAME LEE

The menus at Queen's English are inspired by Hong Kong and the 156 years it spent as a British territory. The bar stocks a selection of baijiu, a clear Chinese liquor that's among the most consumed spirits in the world. In creating this spin on a Daiquiri, bar manager Tracy Eustaquio maintains the classic's clean and balanced profile while pumping up the flavor at every step. If you don't have purple carrots for the juice, regular orange ones will do.

GLASSWARE: Rocks glass

GARNISH: None

- 1½ oz. Pimm's
- ¾ oz. fresh lime juice
- ¾ oz. Simple Syrup (see page 20)
- ½ oz. Jamaican rum
- ½ oz. fresh purple carrot juice
- 1 bar spoon rose water, to float

1. Place all of the ingredients, except for the rose water, in a cocktail shaker, fill it two-thirds of the way with ice, and shake until chilled.

2. Strain the cocktail over ice into the rocks glass. Float the rose water on top of the drink, pouring it over the back of a bar spoon, and enjoy.

OAXACAN BOTTLEROCKET

ROOSTER & OWL
WASHINGTON, D.C.

The Oaxacan Bottlerocket is a tribute to Chris Sang's favorite cocktail, the Queen's Park Swizzle. Rather than using the traditional combination of spiced and overproof rums, Sang opted for similar components with a spice kick from a house-made syrup to pair with a base of mezcal and spiced rum. The spirit-forward drink is served over pebble ice to soften the boozy punch.

GLASSWARE: Collins glass
GARNISH: Fresh mint

- **Handful of fresh mint**
- **¾ oz. Del Maguey Vida Mezcal**
- **¾ oz. Smith & Cross Rum**
- **1 oz. fresh lime juice**
- **¾ oz. Thai Chile & Basil Syrup (see recipe)**
- **½ oz. falernum**
- **½ oz. orange juice**
- **Peychaud's Bitters, to top**

1. Place the fresh mint at the bottom of the Collins glass and fill the glass with pebble ice.

2. Fill the glass with the remaining ingredients, except for the bitters, and top with more pebble ice.

3. Top with bitters until you see a nice red layer on the top of the drink. Garnish with additional fresh mint and enjoy.

THAI CHILE & BASIL SYRUP: Add 10 grams of diced Thai chile pepper and one-quarter of a package of Thai basil to 2 cups of Simple Syrup (see page 20). Let the mixture steep in the refrigerator for 2 days and strain before using or storing.

GOTTA ROLL

BOUNDARY STONE
WASHINGTON, D.C.

Boundary Stone brings a welcoming, warm pub feel to D.C.'s Bloomingdale neighborhood, just a bit north and west of Shaw. The story behind the Gotta Roll, the longest-running cocktail on the bar's menu, centers around longtime friend of the bar R. B. Wolfensberger. Along with his wife, Meghan Brown, Wolfensberger is also the owner and founder of Gray Wolf Craft Distilling in Saint Michaels, Maryland, which makes the gin used in this shaken drink.

GLASSWARE: Coupe

GARNISH: Dehydrated lemon slice

- 1½ oz. Gray Wolf Timber Sassafras Gin
- ½ oz. elderflower liqueur
- ¾ oz. fresh lemon juice
- ¼ oz. Simple Syrup (see page 20)

1. Place all of the ingredients in a cocktail shaker, fill it two-thirds of the way with ice, and shake until chilled.

2. Double-strain the cocktail into the coupe, garnish with the strip of lemon peel, and enjoy.

A STONE'S THROW

BEUCHERT'S SALOON
WASHINGTON, D.C.

Beverage director MacKenzie Conway says this tossed cocktail has off-dry flavors similar to a Manhattan, with a rich texture from the Barolo Chinato, notes of pine and anise from the mastiha, and a boozy rye spice that cuts through both.

GLASSWARE: Coupe
GARNISH: Lemon twist

- 1½ oz. Sazerac 6 Year Rye Whiskey
- ¾ oz. Cocchi Barolo Chinato
- ¾ oz. Skinos Mastiha Spirit Liqueur

1. Place all of the ingredients in a cocktail shaker. Fill another cocktail shaker with ice and place a julep strainer over the top.

2. Pour the mixture into the cocktail shaker containing the ice and then strain it back into the shaker containing no ice. Repeat this tossing process 3 or 4 times until the cocktail is chilled and diluted.

3. Strain the cocktail into the coupe, garnish with the lemon twist, and enjoy.

4 GRAPES

CIEL SOCIAL CLUB
WASHINGTON, D.C.

In this elegant and effervescent cocktail, Versus Hospitality beverage director Hank Bowers finds a way to feature grapes in four different ways: pisco liquor, verjus, a Cava-based syrup, and a delightfully playful foam to top it all off. It's just the right amount of sophistication and whimsy.

GLASSWARE: Nick & Nora glass
GARNISH: Grape Cotton Candy Foam (see recipe)

- 1½ oz. Caravedo Pisco
- 1 oz. Cava Syrup (see recipe)
- 1 oz. verjus

1. Place all of the ingredients in a cocktail shaker, fill it two-thirds of the way with ice, and shake until chilled.

2. Double-strain the cocktail into the Nick & Nora glass, garnish with the Grape Cotton Candy Foam, and enjoy.

GRAPE COTTON CANDY FOAM: In a blender, combine 400 grams grape juice, 2 grams Versawhip (0.5 percent concentration), and 1 gram xanthan gum and puree. Place the blended solution in a medium bowl and foam it with an immersion blender, or place it in a charged whipping gun.

CAVA SYRUP: In a large pot or saucepan, combine 1 quart Cava and 1 quart sugar and bring the mixture to a boil, stirring to dissolve the sugar. Reduce the heat and let the mixture simmer until the volume has reduced by half and the smell of alcohol is gone. Let the syrup cool completely before using or storing in the refrigerator.

ABSINTHE RICKEY

DAUPHINE'S
WASHINGTON, D.C.

The joyous energy of New Orleans runs through all corners of Dauphine's. The restaurant is known for its homemade charcuterie, butchery, and seafood along with a menu of cocktails reminiscent of a night out in the Big Easy. After sipping on a Hurricane or a Sazerac, consider this cocktail, the bar's interpretation of the Rickey, which remains true to the dry and tart original while introducing absinthe and high-quality crème de menthe for a bold and fresh taste.

GLASSWARE: Collins glass
GARNISH: Grated cinnamon

- ½ lime
- ½ oz. Tempus Fugit Crème de Menthe
- 2 oz. Kübler Swiss Absinthe
- 1 oz. Fever-Tree Club Soda

1. Squeeze the lime into the Collins glass and drop the lime shell into the glass.

2. Add the remaining ingredients, fill the glass with pebble ice, and gently swizzle for approximately 5 seconds.

3. Add more pebble ice to the glass, garnish with grated cinnamon, and enjoy.

PRELUDE TO A KISS

ELLINGTON PARK BISTRO
WASHINGTON, D.C.

Paying homage to the 1938 classic ballad composed by Duke Ellington, Taha Ismail, director of food and beverage at the Ellington Park Bistro in the St. Gregory Hotel, wanted to showcase his creative take on a beloved classic sour cocktail.

GLASSWARE: Coupe
GARNISH: None

- 1½ oz. Empress 1908 Gin
- ¾ oz. fresh lime juice
- ½ oz. Dolin Blanc
- ¼ oz. Chambord
- ½ oz. Giffard Crème de Violette
- ½ oz. Lavender Syrup (see recipe)
- ½ oz. egg white

1. Place all of the ingredients in a cocktail shaker and dry shake for 10 seconds.

2. Add ice to the shaker and shake until well chilled.

3. Double-strain the cocktail into the coupe and enjoy.

LAVENDER SYRUP: Combine 250 grams sugar, 250 grams water, and 1.25 grams dried lavender in a saucepan and bring the mixture to a boil over medium heat, stirring to dissolve the sugar. Remove the pan from heat, let the syrup cool completely, and strain before using or storing.

SOUTHEAST

Classic Mob Movie ★ Mai Kinda Gai

Canoe Club ★ The Pink Flamingo

Local Tea Party ★ Lychee Daiquiri

Pillow Talk ★ The Halliwell

Blacker the Berry, the Sweeter the Juice

Wynwood Mule ★ Tom Kyu Gai

Drunken Rabbit ★ Bangkok, Bangkok

Spring in Tokyo ★ Cocoa Puff Old Fashioned

The Banks Sour ★ Karajuku Gimlet

Sayonara! ★ Be My Wine ★ Root Healer

Paomo Ambrosia ★ Dan's Piña Paradise

Tropic Punch ★ The Speck-tacular Now

The Pineapple ★ Go Ahead Romeo

Thyme Traveler ★ Desert Daisy

Rockaway Daiquiri

In the mind, Florida is where America goes to relax, either to shrug off the trappings of adulthood and embrace their inner child at Disney World, or to step away from all responsibility and soak up the sun on the beach while enjoying an endless string a slushy, boozy beverages. And, while this latter, Buffett-inspired image holds true in many spots across the Sunshine State, there is one city where the cocktail connoisseur can be assured of having their needs met: Miami.

Miami is far more cosmopolitan than most may think, and its late-night scene ranks right there with Madrid in terms of intensity and outlandishness. For the industry to keep pace, a top-flight cocktail scene is a must, and Miami's bartenders have more than met that call, proving to be astonishingly good at blending myriad international influences to produce cocktails that are refined and accessible. Under the guidance of the legendary John Lermayer, bartenders in Miami have learned to combine true craft with the playful nature that thrives in the Sunshine State. From drinks that look to the mob movie for inspiration to those that mine nostalgia for the sugary cereals of childhood, Miami proves to be as cutting edge, cool, and cheeky as one would expect from one of the country's hottest cities.

CLASSIC MOB MOVIE

THE ANDERSON
MIAMI, FLORIDA

Miami cocktail dons Gabe Orta and Elad Zvi built another fantastic team at The Anderson, and this Godfather riff from Dave Simmons really stands out.

GLASSWARE: Cocktail glass
GARNISH: Strip of orange peel, Filthy Cherries

- 2 oz. The Glenlivet Founder's Reserve Scotch Whisky
- ½ oz. DeKuyper Amaretto

- 2 dashes of Angostura Bitters
- ½ oz. Martini & Rossi Sweet Vermouth

1. Chill the cocktail glass in the freezer.

2. Place all of the ingredients in a mixing glass, fill it two-thirds of the way with ice, and stir until chilled.

3. Strain the cocktail into the chilled glass. Express the strip of orange peel over the cocktail, garnish the drink with it and the cherries, and enjoy.

MAI KINDA GAI

THE ANDERSON
MIAMI, FLORIDA

This is Miami's Mai Tai! Made with an inventive orgeat, this is one boozy, citrusy, complex drink.

★

GLASSWARE: Rocks glass
GARNISH: Fresh mint, orange slice, maraschino cherry

- ¾ oz. Banana & Cashew Orgeat (see recipe)
- 1½ oz. Hamilton 86 Rum
- ½ oz. Mandarine Napoléon
- 1 oz. fresh lime juice
- ½ oz. Ron Zacapa 23 Rum, to float

1. Place all of the ingredients, except for the Ron Zacapa, in a cocktail shaker, fill it two-thirds of the way with ice, and shake until chilled.

2. Fill the rocks glass with ice and strain the cocktail over it.

3. Float the Ron Zacapa on top of the drink, pouring it slowly over the back of a spoon.

4. Garnish with the fresh mint, orange slice, and maraschino cherry and enjoy.

BANANA & CASHEW ORGEAT: In a saucepan, bring 1 cup of cashew milk to a simmer. Place 2 cups of sugar in a container, pour the warmed milk over it, and stir until the sugar has dissolved. Let the mixture cool completely and then stir in 4 oz. of Giffard Banane du Brésil. Use immediately or store in the refrigerator.

CANOE CLUB

CASA FLORIDA
MIAMI, FLORIDA

This cocktail brings out the delicate smoky notes of mezcal while staying tropical and fruity. A great drink for both mezcal lovers and those wanting to experiment more with the spirit.

GLASSWARE: Rocks glass
GARNISH: None

- 1½ oz. mezcal
- ½ oz. crème de mure
- ¾ oz. Ginger & Serrano Syrup (see recipe)

- ½ oz. fresh lime juice
- 3 dashes of Peychaud's Bitters

1. Place all of the ingredients in a cocktail shaker, stir to combine, fill the shaker two-thirds of the way with ice, and shake vigorously until chilled.

2. Fill the rocks glass with crushed or pebble ice, strain the cocktail over it, and enjoy.

GINGER & SERRANO SYRUP: Place 2 cups sugar, 1 cup water, 3 chopped serrano chile peppers, and 2 large chopped pieces of ginger in a saucepan and bring to a simmer, stirring to dissolve the sugar. Cook for 10 minutes and strain the syrup into a mason jar. Let the syrup cool completely before using or storing in the refrigerator.

THE PINK FLAMINGO

CASA FLORIDA
MIAMI, FLORIDA

We are all suckers for a nice frozen cocktail. This riff on the Piña Colada combines floral flavors, tea, and coconut and ties them together with a Fernet-Branca reduction. Whoa!

GLASSWARE: Footed pilsner glass
GARNISH: Edible flower blossom

- **Splash of Fernet-Branca Reduction (see recipe)**
- **1½ oz. Banks 5 Island Rum**
- **½ oz. Pineapple Syrup (see page 90)**
- **1 oz. freshly brewed hibiscus tea**
- **½ oz. condensed milk**
- **½ oz. cream of coconut**

1. Place the reduction in the pilsner glass and set it aside.
2. Place the remaining ingredients and ½ cup ice in a blender and puree until smooth.
3. Pour the contents of the blender into the glass, garnish with the edible flower blossom, and enjoy.

FERNET-BRANCA REDUCTION: In a saucepan, combine equal parts Fernet-Branca and sugar and cook until the mixture is syrupy. Remove the pan from heat and let the reduction cool completely before using or storing.

LOCAL TEA PARTY

THE LOCAL CRAFT FOOD & DRINK
MIAMI, FLORIDA

Barbara Peña Mehnert had Miami's incredible bounty of local ingredients in mind when she decided to use honey and lychee for this tropical tea cocktail, which you'll want to drink all summer.

GLASSWARE: Vintage teacup
GARNISH: None

- 2 oz. The Botanist Islay Dry Gin
- ¾ oz. Lychee-Infused Honey (see recipe)
- ¾ oz. fresh lemon juice
- ¼ oz. Blackberry-Infused Salers Aperitif (see recipe)
- 1 sprig of fresh rosemary
- 1 bar spoon Green Chartreuse

1. Place the gin, honey, lemon juice, and infused aperitif in a cocktail shaker, fill it two-thirds of the way with ice, and shake vigorously until chilled.

2. Place the fresh rosemary sprig in the teacup, add the spoonful of Chartreuse, and use a wand lighter or a long match to ignite the Chartreuse.

3. Double-strain the cocktail into the teacup and enjoy.

LYCHEE-INFUSED HONEY: Place 2 cups chopped lychees, 1 cup local honey, and 1 cup water in a saucepan and bring to a simmer over low heat. Cook for 30 minutes. Remove the pan from heat and let the mixture steep for 3 hours. Strain before using or storing.

BLACKBERRY-INFUSED SALERS APERITIF: Place 2 pints of fresh blackberries and a 750 ml bottle of Salers Aperitif in a large mason jar and steep for 1 week. Strain before using or storing.

LYCHEE DAIQUIRI

1-800-LUCKY
MIAMI, FLORIDA

There's nothing like a hand-shaken Daiquiri when you're in Miami. Add a bit of Lychee Syrup and it's a complete game changer.

GLASSWARE: Coupe
GARNISH: Lime wheel

- 2 oz. unaged rum

- 2 dashes of Bittercube Jamaican No. 2 Bitters

- 1 oz. fresh lime juice

- ¾ oz. Lychee Syrup (see recipe)

1. Place all of the ingredients in a cocktail shaker, fill it two-thirds of the way with ice, and shake until chilled.

2. Strain into the coupe, garnish with the lime wheel, and enjoy.

LYCHEE SYRUP: Remove the skins and seeds from ½ lb. of lychees, place them in a blender, and puree until smooth. Pour the puree into a saucepan, add 1 cup sugar and 1 cup water, and cook over medium heat, stirring to dissolve the sugar. Cook until the desired consistency is achieved. Remove the pan from heat and let the syrup cool completely. Strain before using or storing in the refrigerator.

PILLOW TALK

BAR ALTER
MIAMI, FLORIDA

The botanicals in the gin play off the dandelion bitters in this floral cocktail, and the apple air elevates the drink.

GLASSWARE: Rocks glass or Irish coffee mug
GARNISH: Edible flower blossoms, spritz of absinthe

- 2 oz. Martin Miller's Gin
- ½ oz. Gran Classico Bitter
- ½ oz. Simple Syrup (see page 20)
- ½ oz. fresh lemon juice
- 3 dashes of Dr. Adam Elmegirab's Dandelion & Burdock Bitters
- Apple Air (see recipe)

1. Place all of the ingredients, except for the Apple Air, in a cocktail shaker, fill it two-thirds of the way with ice, and shake until chilled.

2. Strain the cocktail over ice into the glass and layer the Apple Air on top.

3. Garnish with edible flower blossoms and a spritz of absinthe and enjoy.

APPLE AIR: Place 1¼ cups fresh apple juice, ¼ teaspoon citric acid, ¼ teaspoon salt, ½ teaspoon sugar, 1 teaspoon xanthan gum, and ½ oz. Versawhip in a bowl and foam with an immersion blender.

THE HALLIWELL

BEAKER & GRAY
MIAMI, FLORIDA

Ben Potts knows there is nothing like strawberries and mint in Miami's heat, which is why he put them in this refreshing vodka cocktail.

GLASSWARE: Collins glass
GARNISH: Fresh mint

- 1½ oz. Stoli Vodka
- ½ oz. Cocchi Rosa Americano
- 1 oz. Ginger Syrup (see recipe)
- 1 oz. fresh lemon juice
- 1 oz. strawberry puree
- 8 fresh mint leaves

1. Place all of the ingredients in a cocktail shaker, fill it two-thirds of the way with ice, and shake vigorously until chilled.

2. Double-strain over ice into the Collins glass, garnish with additional fresh mint, and enjoy.

GINGER SYRUP: Place 1 cup water and 1 cup sugar in a saucepan and bring the mixture to a boil, stirring to dissolve the sugar. Add a peeled 1-inch piece of fresh ginger, remove the pan from heat, and let the syrup cool completely. Strain before using or storing.

BLACKER THE BERRY, THE SWEETER THE JUICE

COYO TACO
MIAMI, FLORIDA

★drink that sings with picante and sugary notes, perfect for an evening when you're looking to turn taco night into a memorable occasion.

★

GLASSWARE: Collins glass
GARNISH: Lime wheel, fresh sage

- **5 blackberries**
- **1½ oz. mezcal**
- **¾ oz. St-Germain**
- **½ oz. Ginger Syrup (see page 129)**

- **2 dashes of Bittermens Hellfire Habanero Shrub**
- **¾ oz. fresh lime juice**
- **½ oz. agave nectar**

1. Place the blackberries in the Collins glass, muddle, and top with crushed ice.

2. Place the remaining ingredients in a cocktail shaker, fill it two-thirds of the way with ice, and shake until chilled.

3. Strain the cocktail into the Collins glass, garnish with the lime wheel and sage leaves, and enjoy.

WYNWOOD MULE

KYU

MIAMI, FLORIDA

KYU in Wynwood is responsible for some of Miami's artiest cocktails, and the addition of smoked pineapple makes this mule a masterpiece.

★

GLASSWARE: Copper cup
GARNISH: Pineapple leaf, dehydrated lime wheel

- 1½ oz. vodka
- 1 oz. fresh lime juice
- ¾ oz. Smoked Pineapple Syrup (see recipe)
- 2 oz. ginger beer

1. Place all of the ingredients in the copper cup, fill it with crushed ice, and gently stir.

2. Garnish with the pineapple leaf and dehydrated lime wheel and enjoy.

SMOKED PINEAPPLE SYRUP: Place 4 to 6 whole pineapples in a smoker, set it to 220°F, and smoke the pineapples until they are charred, 3 to 4 hours. Remove from the smoker and let them cool. Chop the pineapples, making sure to reserve any juices, and weigh them. Place the pineapples and any juices in a saucepan and add 60 percent of their weight in water. Bring to a rolling boil and cook for 15 minutes. Stir in 40 percent of the pineapples' weight in sugar and simmer for 45 minutes. Place the mixture in a food processor and blitz until pureed. Strain the syrup and let it cool completely before using or storing. If you're looking for a quicker way to get a smoky flavor into pineapple, slice the pineapples and cook them on a charcoal grill for 15 minutes. Remove them from the grill and follow the same method recommended above.

TOM KYU GAI

KYU
MIAMI, FLORIDA

This is one of the more complex and unique cocktails to come out of Miami's cocktail explosion. It is served warm and the blend of cilantro, chili oil, and the botanicals in the gin fuse for an exotic experience.

GLASSWARE: Porcelain bowl
GARNISH: None

- 1½ oz. Bombay Dry Gin
- ¼ oz. fresh lime juice
- 3 oz. Soup Batch (see recipe)
- 1 bar spoon Cilantro Foam (see recipe)

- 1 fresh cilantro leaf
- 1 dehydrated lime slice
- 5 to 7 drops of chili oil

1. Place the gin, lime juice, and Soup Batch in the porcelain bowl and stir to combine.

2. Top with the Cilantro Foam, cilantro leaf, dehydrated lime slice, and chili oil and enjoy.

SOUP BATCH: Place 135 oz. unsweetened coconut milk, 15 cups coconut water, 2¾ cups freshly pressed galangal juice, 1¾ cups galanagal root debris (left from juicing, wrapped in cheesecloth), 1¼ cups thinly sliced lemongrass, 1¼ cups chicken broth, 1 tablespoon kosher salt, 1 tablespoon kaffir lime leaves, and 2¾ cups Scallion Syrup (see recipe) in a saucepan and bring to a boil. Simmer for 1 hour, remove the pan from heat, and let the mixture cool slightly. Strain before using or storing.

SCALLION SYRUP: Place 4 cups water, 8 cups sugar, and ½ cup minced scallions in a saucepan and bring to a boil, stirring to dissolve the sugar. Remove the pan from heat and let the mixture steep for 15 minutes. Strain the syrup and let it cool completely before using or storing.

CILANTRO FOAM: Place 1 tablespoon sucrose esters and ¾ cup Cilantro Water (see recipe) in a bowl and whisk with an electric frother until foamy.

CILANTRO WATER: Place 4 oz. fresh cilantro and 5¼ cups water in a blender and puree until smooth. Strain before using or storing.

DRUNKEN RABBIT

TAQUIZA
MIAMI, FLORIDA

Sipping from a pineapple will have anyone going tropical, especially if you are on the beach in Miami.

★

GLASSWARE: Emptied pineapple
GARNISH: Pineapple leaves, orange slices, fresh mint,
Tajín, cocktail umbrella

- 2 oz. mezcal
- 1 oz. Ancho Reyes
- 1½ oz. pineapple juice
- 1½ oz. guava juice
- 1 oz. Cinnamon Syrup (see recipe)

1. Place all of the ingredients in a blender, add 2 oz. crushed ice, and puree until smooth.

2. Pour the cocktail into the pineapple shell, garnish with the pineapple leaves, orange slices, fresh mint, Tajín, and cocktail umbrella, and enjoy.

CINNAMON SYRUP: Place 1 cup water and 2 cinnamon sticks in a saucepan and bring the mixture to a boil. Add 2 cups sugar and stir until it has dissolved. Remove the pan from heat, cover it, and let the mixture steep at room temperature for 12 hours. Strain the syrup through cheesecloth before using or storing.

BANGKOK, BANGKOK

27 RESTAURANT & BAR
MIAMI, FLORIDA

Inspired by a restaurant that served Thai teas, 27 relies on a mid-16th century Japanese cold-brew coffee maker to produce the Rye & Tea Infusion. At home, a pour-over coffee maker will do the job.

GLASSWARE: Collins glass
GARNISH: Fresh herbs

- 1½ oz. Rye & Tea Infusion (see recipe)
- ¾ oz. Thai Tea Reduction (see recipe)
- ½ oz. Meletti Amaro

- 1½ oz. coconut cream
- 2 dashes of Bittermens Hopped Grapefruit Bitters
- Toasted autumn spices, to top

1. Place all of the ingredients, except for the autumn spices, in a cocktail shaker, fill it two-thirds of the way with ice, and shake until chilled.

2. Fill the Collins glass with crushed ice and strain the cocktail over it.

3. Top with the autumn spices, garnish with your preferred fresh herbs, and enjoy.

RYE & TEA INFUSION: Line a pour-over coffee maker with a paper filter and place loose-leaf Thai tea, hazelnuts, autumn spices, and dried cranberry hibiscus blossoms in the filter. Slowly pour rye whiskey and then Meletti over the mixture and use as desired.

THAI TEA REDUCTION: Place 1½ cups sugar and 1 cup water in a saucepan, add 1½ teaspoons loose-leaf Thai tea, and bring to a simmer. Cook until the mixture has reduced, stirring occasionally to dissolve the sugar. Remove the pan from heat and let the reduction cool completely. Strain before using or storing.

SPRING IN TOKYO

The shochu in this recipe is made with rice and lemongrass local to Miami. When paired with yuzu juice and the bitter-plum flavor of the umeshu, it makes for a sublime drink.

GLASSWARE: Rocks glass

GARNISH: None

- ¾ oz. Mizu Lemongrass Shochu
- ¾ oz. umeshu
- ½ oz. fresh yuzu juice
- ½ oz. Simple Syrup (see page 20)
- ½ oz. egg white

1. Place all of the ingredients in a cocktail shaker, fill it two-thirds of the way with ice, and shake until chilled.

2. Strain the cocktail into a glass, discard the ice, and return the cocktail to the shaker. Dry shake for 10 seconds.

3. Strain over an ice sphere into the rocks glass and enjoy.

COCOA PUFF OLD FASHIONED

BROKEN SHAKER
MIAMI, FLORIDA

Cocoa Puff–Infused Bourbon reinvents the Old Fashioned. The chocolate and bourbon become best friends in this decadent yet balanced drink. A modern classic from one of the very best bars in the world.

GLASSWARE: Rocks glass
GARNISH: Strip of orange peel

- 2 oz. Cocoa Puff–Infused Bourbon (see recipe)
- 5 drops of white soy sauce
- 2 dashes of Bittermens Xocolatl Mole Bitters
- ¼ oz. Simple Syrup (see page 20)

1. Place all of the ingredients in a mixing glass, fill it two-thirds of the way with ice, and stir until chilled.
2. Strain over a large ice cube into the rocks glass, garnish with the strip of orange peel, and enjoy.

COCOA PUFF–INFUSED BOURBON: Place 1 box of Cocoa Puffs and a 750 ml bottle of bourbon in a large container and let the mixture steep for 1 day. Strain before using or storing.

SAGE & ROSEMARY TINCTURE: Add the leaves from 5 sprigs of sage and 5 sprigs of rosemary to 1 cup vodka. Let the mixture steep for 3 days and strain before using or storing.

CHERRY & CIDER FOAM: In a saucepan, combine 3 cups pitted cherries and 12 oz. Crispin Rosé Hard Cider and simmer over low heat for 20 minutes. Strain and let the liquid cool completely. Add 1 teaspoon Versawhip and place the mixture in a charged whipping gun.

THE BANKS SOUR

When sipping this drink, whiffs of a bakery will hit you, thanks to the Coconut-Washed Rum, Dry Spice Syrup, and Cherry & Cider Foam.

★

GLASSWARE: Nick & Nora glass
GARNISH: Fresh rosemary

- **1½ oz. Coconut-Washed Rum (see recipe)**
- **¾ oz. fresh lime juice**
- **½ oz. Dry Spice Syrup (see recipe)**

- **5 drops of Sage & Rosemary Tincture (see recipe)**
- **½ oz. Cava**
- **Cherry & Cider Foam, to top (see recipe)**

1. Chill the Nick & Nora glass in the freezer.

2. Place the rum, lime juice, syrup, and tincture in a cocktail shaker, fill it two-thirds of the way with ice, and shake until chilled.

3. Add the Cava to the shaker and double-strain the cocktail into the chilled glass.

4. Layer the foam on top of the drink, garnish with the fresh rosemary, and enjoy.

COCONUT-WASHED RUM: In a large bowl, combine ½ cup unrefined coconut oil with a 750 ml bottle of Banks 7 Golden Age Rum. Stir until well combined and place the rum in the freezer overnight. Remove the hardened layer of fat, strain the rum through a coffee filter, and use as desired.

DRY SPICE SYRUP: In a saucepan, bring 2 cups of water to a boil and add 3 cinnamon sticks, 3 whole cloves, and 1 star anise pod. Remove from heat and cover the pan for 3 minutes. Add 3 cups sugar, stir to dissolve, and let the syrup cool completely. Strain before using or storing.

KARAJUKU GIMLET

KAIDO
MIAMI, FLORIDA

This beauty from Nico de Soto features the delicately floral kaffir lime cordial playing well with the green tea–infused Mizu Lemongrass Shochu, making for a gorgeously simple and delightful cocktail.

★

GLASSWARE: Japanese teacup
GARNISH: Kaffir lime leaves

- **1½ oz. Green Tea–Infused Shochu (see recipe)**
- **¾ oz. Kaffir Lime Cordial (see recipe)**

1. Place all of the ingredients in a mixing glass, fill it two-thirds of the way with ice, and stir until chilled.

2. Strain into the teacup, garnish with the lime leaves, and enjoy.

GREEN TEA–INFUSED SHOCHU: Place a 750 ml bottle of Mizu Lemongrass Shochu and 1 oz. loose-leaf green tea in a large mason jar and steep for 8 minutes. Strain before using or storing.

KAFFIR LIME CORDIAL: Place 4 cups water, 1¼ cups sugar, 2 teaspoons tartaric acid, 1 teaspoon malic acid, and a dash of citric acid in a saucepan and cook over medium heat until the mixture is well combined. Remove the pan from heat and let the cordial cool before using or storing.

SAYONARA!

This whisky cocktail makes clear why Nico de Soto is an award-winning bartender. The complex Asian-inspired flavors deliver bold umami that lives up to the cocktail's name. Ichijiku are Japanese figs, and kuromitsu is a Japanese sugar syrup whose name translates to "black honey." Both can be found online, or at well-stocked Asian markets.

GLASSWARE: Rocks glass
GARNISH: Sliced ichijiku

- **2 oz. Ichijiku-Infused Whisky (see recipe)**
- **5 drops of white soy sauce**
- **2 dashes of Kombu & Nori Bitters (see recipe)**
- **⅓ oz. Licorice Kuromitsu (see recipe)**

1. Place all of the ingredients in a mixing glass, fill it two-thirds of the way with ice, and stir until chilled.

2. Strain over ice into the rocks glass, garnish with the sliced ichijiku, and enjoy.

ICHIJIKU-INFUSED WHISKY: Placed 5 halved ichijiku and a 750 ml bottle of Nikka Whisky From the Barrel in a vacuum bag, seal it, and sous vide at 122°F for 1 hour. Remove the bag from the water bath and let the mixture cool. Strain before using or storing.

KOMBU & NORI BITTERS: Place a pinch of nori, a dash of kombu, and a 6.7 oz. bottle of Angostura Bitters in a vacuum bag, seal it, and sous vide at 126.5°F for 2 hours. Remove the bag from the water bath and let the mixture cool. Strain before using or storing.

LICORICE KUROMITSU: Place 5 licorice roots and 4 cups kuromitsu in a large mason jar and store in a cool, dark place for 2 weeks. Strain before using or storing.

BE MY WINE

HABITAT BY JOSE MENDIN
MIAMI, FLORIDA

★

Light-bodied rum provides a great base for this exotic cocktail, which is defined by floral notes, spiced citrus from the falernum, and the inimitable White Wine Reduction.

———————————— ★ ————————————

GLASSWARE: Brandy snifter
GARNISH: Edible flower blossoms

- 1½ oz. Don Q rum
- ¾ oz. White Wine Reduction (see recipe)
- ¾ oz. falernum
- Spritz of lavender oil

1. Place all of the ingredients in a mixing glass, fill it two-thirds of the way with ice, and stir until chilled.

2. Double-strain the cocktail into the brandy snifter, garnish with edible flower blossoms, and enjoy.

WHITE WINE REDUCTION: Place 1 cup dry white wine and ½ cup sugar in a saucepan and bring to a simmer. Cook until the mixture has reduced by half, remove the pan from heat, and let the reduction cool completely before using or storing in the refrigerator.

ROOT HEALER

HAKKASAN
MIAMI, FLORIDA

The Root Healer's complex yet delicate Asian-inspired flavors of passion fruit, pear, and tamarind serve as the perfect complement to Hakkasan's incredible Cantonese cuisine.

GLASSWARE: Coupe

GARNISH: None

- **Smoked salt, for the rim**
- **1½ oz. pear vodka**
- **¼ oz. Calvados VSOP**
- **¼ oz. Asian pear puree**
- **1 oz. tamarind nectar**
- **¼ oz. Passion Fruit Syrup (see recipe)**
- **¼ oz. fresh lime juice**
- **2 fresh shiso leaves**
- **½ oz. Simple Syrup (see page 20)**

1. Wet the rim of the coupe and coat it with smoked salt.

2. Add all of the remaining ingredients to a cocktail shaker, fill it two-thirds of the way with ice, and shake until chilled.

3. Double-strain the cocktail into the coupe and enjoy.

PASSION FRUIT SYRUP: Place 1½ cups passion fruit puree and 1½ cups Demerara Syrup (see page 63) in a mason jar, seal it, and shake until combined. Use immediately or store in the refrigerator.

PAOMO AMBROSIA

HAKKASAN
MIAMI, FLORIDA

The cachaça and sake combined with yuzu juice and banana make this complex cocktail effortless to consume.

★

GLASSWARE: Rocks glass
GARNISH: Finely ground white ambrosia tea leaves

- 1½ oz. cachaça
- ½ oz. sake
- 1 oz. Banana Syrup (see recipe)
- ½ oz. yuzu juice
- ¼ oz. fresh lemon juice
- 2 crushed shiso leaves
- 1 egg white
- Club soda, to top

1. Place all of the ingredients, except for the club soda, in a cocktail shaker and dry shake for 10 seconds.
2. Add ice, shake until chilled, and double-strain the cocktail over ice into the rocks glass.
3. Top with club soda, garnish with the ground tea leaves, and enjoy.

BANANA SYRUP: Place 5 peeled bananas and 4 cups Simple Syrup (see page 20) in a saucepan and bring to a boil. Cook for 5 minutes, reduce the heat to medium-low, and simmer for 15 minutes. Strain the syrup and let it cool completely before using or storing.

DAN'S PIÑA PARADISE

ESOTICO MIAMI
MIAMI, FLORIDA

Daniele Dalla Pola dug into the history books for this tiki beauty—the original recipe for the cocktail comes from Sam Denning of Club Luau, a popular spot in Miami during the 1950s.

GLASSWARE: Brandy snifter
GARNISH: Cinnamon, strip of orange peel

- 2 oz. Diplomatico Reserva Rum
- ½ oz. Plantation Stiggins' Fancy Pineapple Rum
- ½ oz. fresh lime juice
- ½ oz. fresh grapefruit juice
- ½ oz. fresh orange juice
- 1 oz. #9 (see recipe)
- 4 pineapple chunks

1. Place the ingredients in a blender, add ½ cup ice, and puree until smooth.

2. Pour the cocktail into the brandy snifter, garnish with the cinnamon and orange peel, and enjoy.

#9: Place 2 oz. Reàl ginger syrup and 1 oz. almond paste in a container and stir until combined. Stir in 1 teaspoon St. Elizabeth Allspice Dram and use immediately or store in the refrigerator.

TROPIC PUNCH

LIVING ROOM AT THE W HOTEL
MIAMI, FLORIDA

The tropical flavors of this punch are right at home on the sands of Miami Beach.

★

GLASSWARE: Collins glass
GARNISH: Dehydrated orange wheel, pineapple leaf

- 2 oz. aged rum
- ½ oz. Aperol
- 1 oz. pineapple juice
- 1 oz. orange juice
- ¾ oz. fresh lime juice
- ¾ oz. agave nectar
- Dash of egg white

1. Place all of the ingredients in a cocktail shaker, fill it two-thirds of the way with ice, and shake until chilled.

2. Strain over ice into the Collins glass, garnish with the dehydrated orange wheel and pineapple leaf, and enjoy.

THE SPECK-TACULAR NOW

MACCHIALINA
MIAMI, FLORIDA

You had me at speck! This take on an Old Fashioned features speck-infused bourbon, which plays well with the playful complexity of the sweet-and-spicy syrup.

GLASSWARE: Rocks glass
GARNISH: Strip of orange peel

- **2 oz. Speck-Washed Bourbon (see recipe)**
- **Dash of Bittercube Jamaican No. 1 Bitters**

- **½ oz. Honey & Clove Syrup (see recipe)**

1. Place all of the ingredients in a mixing glass, fill it two-thirds of the way with ice, and stir until chilled.

2. Strain over ice into the rocks glass, garnish with the strip of orange peel, and enjoy.

SPECK-WASHED BOURBON: Place speck in a skillet and warm it over medium-low heat until the fat has rendered. Add 8 oz. of rendered fat and a 750 ml bottle of bourbon to a vacuum bag, seal it, and sous vide at 155°F for 1½ hours. Transfer the mixture to a large mason jar and freeze it over overnight. Remove the layer of hardened fat and strain the bourbon through a coffee filter.

HONEY & CLOVE SYRUP: In a saucepan, combine 2 cups honey and 2 cups water and bring to a boil, stirring to combine. Remove the pan from heat, add 25 whole cloves, and let the mixture steep at room temperature until it cools completely. Strain the syrup before using or storing.

THE PINEAPPLE

MATADOR ROOM AT THE EDITION HOTEL
MIAMI, FLORIDA

The Pineapple, defined by the bespoke Pineapple Mix, is one of the Matador Room's signature cocktails, and is served in a stunningly beautiful vessel.

★

GLASSWARE: Copper cup
GARNISH: Torched sprig of fresh rosemary

- 2½ oz. Absolut Elyx Vodka
- 2 oz. Pineapple Mix (see recipe)
- 1 oz. pineapple puree
- ¾ oz. fresh lemon juice
- Peychaud's Bitters, to top

1. Place all of the ingredients, except for the bitters, in a cocktail shaker, fill it two-thirds of the way with ice, and shake until chilled.

2. Fill the copper cup with crushed ice and strain the cocktail over it.

3. Top with more crushed ice and drizzle bitters over the cocktail.

4. Garnish with the torched sprig of fresh rosemary and enjoy.

PINEAPPLE MIX: Place 1¼ cups oloroso sherry, ½ cup Salted Vanilla Syrup (see recipe), 1 cup Rosemary Syrup (see recipe), ½ cup pineapple puree, ½ cup Simple Syrup (see page 20), and ½ bottle Bittermens 'Elemakule Tiki Bitters in a mason jar and stir to combine. Use immediately or store in the refrigerator.

SALTED VANILLA SYRUP: Place 3 pinches of salt, 2 cups Simple Syrup, and 1 tablespoon pure vanilla extract in a saucepan and bring to a simmer, stirring to dissolve the salt. Remove the pan from heat and let the syrup cool completely before using or storing.

ROSEMARY SYRUP: Place 1 cup water in a saucepan and bring to a boil. Add 1 cup sugar and 4 sprigs of fresh rosemary and stir until the sugar has dissolved. Remove the pan from heat and let the syrup cool completely. Strain before using or storing.

GO AHEAD ROMEO

STRIPSTEAK BY MICHAEL MINA
MIAMI, FLORIDA

Aperol almost glows when it's frozen, and as it starts to melt its citrus notes add another layer to the cocktail. Don't hesitate to try these ice cubes in other cocktails as well.

★

GLASSWARE: Brandy snifter
GARNISH: Orange twist

- **6 Aperol Ice Cubes (see recipe)**
- **4 oz. Prosecco**

1. Place the Aperol Ice Cubes in the snifter and pour the Prosecco over them.

2. Garnish with the orange twist and enjoy.

APEROL ICE CUBES: Combine ¼ cup Aperol and ¾ cup water, pour the mixture into ice cube trays, and freeze until solid.

THYME TRAVELER

STUBBORN SEED
MIAMI, FLORIDA

This drink tastes like summer, with gin, elderflower, and cucumber combined with citrus and spicy bitters. The Thyme Syrup ties it all together, highlighting the botanicals in the gin.

GLASSWARE: Collins glass
GARNISH: Sprig of fresh thyme

- 1 cucumber ribbon
- 1½ oz. Bombay Dry Gin
- ½ oz. St-Germain
- ¾ oz. freshly pressed cucumber juice
- ½ oz. Thyme Syrup (see recipe)
- ½ oz. fresh lemon juice
- Dash of Bittermens Hellfire Habanero Shrub

1. Place all of the ingredients in a cocktail shaker, fill it two-thirds of the way with ice, and shake vigorously until chilled.

2. Strain over ice into the Collins glass, garnish with the fresh thyme, and enjoy.

THYME SYRUP: Place 1 cup water, 1 cup sugar, and 1 small bundle of fresh thyme in a saucepan and bring to a boil, stirring to dissolve the sugar. Remove the pan from heat and let the mixture steep for 1 hour. Strain and let the syrup cool completely before using or storing.

DESERT DAISY

STUBBORN SEED
MIAMI, FLORIDA

A stunning tequila cocktail that does not need a gorgeous handmade glass in order to wow someone, but is so imaginative and well executed that it deserves such trappings.

GLASSWARE: Jakobsen glass or rocks glass
GARNISH: Carrot & Habanero Powder (see recipe), edible flower blossom

- 1½ oz. Olmeca Altos Tequila
- ½ oz. BROVO Amaro #4
- ¾ oz. fresh lime juice
- ¾ oz. Bell Pepper & Beet Syrup (see recipe)
- 4 drops of 25 Percent Saline Solution (see recipe)
- 10 dashes of Bittermens Hellfire Habanero Shrub

1. Place all of the ingredients in a cocktail shaker, fill it two-thirds of the way with ice, and shake until chilled.

2. Strain the cocktail over ice into the chosen glass, garnish with the Carrot & Habanero Powder and flower blossom, and enjoy.

BELL PEPPER & BEET SYRUP: Juice ½ cup chopped orange bell pepper and ½ cup chopped beets separately and strain to remove any remaining pulp. Place the juices in a saucepan, add 1 cup sugar, and bring to a boil. Reduce heat so that the mixture simmers and stir until the sugar has dissolved. Remove the pan from heat and let the syrup cool completely before using or storing.

25 PERCENT SALINE SOLUTION: Place 1 oz. of salt in a measuring cup. Add warm water until you reach 4 oz. and the salt has dissolved. Let the solution cool before using or storing.

CARROT & HABANERO POWDER: Use a mortar and pestle to grind 2 tablespoons dehydrated carrots, 2 tablespoons red pepper flakes, and 2 tablespoons kosher salt into a fine powder.

ROCKAWAY DAIQUIRI

SWEET LIBERTY DRINKS & SUPPLY CO.
MIAMI, FLORIDA

John Lermayer, with the help of barman Nick Nistico, devised what could be the best Daiquiri on the planet. The texture, the balance, the taste, the aroma—it's all spot-on. A perfect Miami sipper.

GLASSWARE: Coupe
GARNISH: Dusting of nutmeg

- 1 oz. aged Jamaican rum
- 1 oz. Venezuelan rum
- 2 oz. fresh pineapple juice
- ¾ oz. Licor 43
- ½ oz. agave nectar
- 2 drops of aromatic bitters

1. Place all of the ingredients in a cocktail shaker, fill it two-thirds of the way with ice, and shake until chilled.

2. Double-strain into the coupe, garnish with the dusting of nutmeg, and enjoy.

IN MEMORIAM
JOHN LERMAYER (1963-2018)

Over the course of Miami cocktail history, no one has had more of an impact than John Lermayer. He helped champion the cocktail revival in Miami that brought fresh ingredients, incredible cocktails, and amazing bartenders to this growing community. It is impossible to summarize his contributions to the Miami cocktail scene here, as his legacy deserves a book of its own.

John came to Miami to bartend at the SkyBar at the Shore Club. His bar had fresh ingredients (an uncommon sight in Miami at the time), and his seamless style behind the bar would carry throughout his career. When he led the bar team at The Florida Room, guests were drinking Mules, Manhattans, and Old Fashioneds—forgotten cocktails in Miami's bars and restaurants at the time.

Many hospitality professionals mark John's time at The Florida Room as a turning point in Miami's cocktail revolution. John's bottomless thirst for knowledge led him all over the world, meeting bartenders and ambassadors who would come to Miami and return the favor. John was a great leader in the world of spirits, and his colleagues recognized that. John, along with his trusted bar team, went on to open the award-winning Regent Cocktail Club, which championed classic cocktails on its menu. After his stint at The Regent Cocktail Club, he turned his attention to his masterwork, Sweet Liberty. His work and mentorship quickly brought Sweet Liberty worldwide recognition and numerous awards.

John always went out of his way to make people feel welcome, and he helped give Miami a place at the table with other major cocktail destinations. He will be remembered as an incredible bartender, a trusted educator and mentor, a loving father, and a devoted friend.

SOUTH

Sazerac ★ Vieux Carre
Crazy Town ★ Ramos Gin Fizz
Grasshopper ★ Cade's Cove
Rollo Raiders ★ Molokai Mishap
Bridesmaid's Tears ★ L & N
Little Black Star
Drink of Laughter and Forgetting
Magic Tree ★ Quarter Tank of Gasoline
Fjordian Slip ★ Nertz!
No True Scotsman ★ Gunshop Fizz
Official Drink of Nashville
King Cake Milkshake
Classic Hurricane ★ Strange Brew

After riding the wave of Miami's incredible energy through a series of late nights, one will no doubt be in need of a place to recuperate. Fortunately, the next stop on our tour, New Orleans, is perhaps the best place in the entire United States to take a step back and let the chips fall where they may.

As Bob Dylan once said, "I like a lot of places. But I like New Orleans better." Anyone who has spent any time there understands why—simply put, the Crescent City is a unique blend of style, elegance, playfulness, tradition, openness, and myriad other characteristics that evade description. If you spend a week there and it doesn't instantly inhabit your list of favorite places, you're the problem. No small piece of the town's charm is its early embrace of the cocktail, no doubt due to its ability to foster the le bon temps roule spirit New Orleans is after. The birthplace of seminal drinks such as the Sazerac, Grasshopper, Hurricane, and Ramos Gin Fizz, cocktail culture in the Big Easy has always been strong.

Our trip through the South also takes us through America's latest boomtown, Nashville. Though it has always been a destination thanks to being the home of one of the truly great American exports, country music, over the course of the last decade people have discovered what a great city it is, and started moving there in droves. As you might imagine, where the crowds flock the restaurant and bars soon follow, and some of the very best cocktails to come out of this boom are gathered here.

SAZERAC

At times, it feels like you can't go 2 feet in New Orleans without a bartender giving you the in-depth history of the city's golden cocktail, the Sazerac. Believed (erroneously) by many New Orleanians to have been the first-ever cocktail, the Sazerac might not have pioneered the mixed drink—I mean, come on, folks figured that out long ago—but it certainly raised the bar.

GLASSWARE: Rocks glass

GARNISH: Strip of lemon peel

- **2 sugar cubes**
- **1¼ oz. Herbsaint**
- **5 to 7 dashes of Peychaud's Bitters**
- **2 oz. rye whiskey**

1. Fill the rocks glass with ice.

2. Place the sugar cubes in a mixing glass, add ¾ oz. of the Herbsaint and the bitters, and muddle.

3. Add the rye, muddle to combine, and add ice. Stir until chilled.

4. Empty the ice from the rocks glass, coat the glass with the remaining Herbsaint, and swirl to rinse the glass. Discard the excess Herbsaint and strain the contents of the mixing glass into the rocks glass.

5. Garnish with the strip of lemon peel and enjoy.

VIEUX CARRE

NEW ORLEANS, LOUISIANA

S ome believe the Vieux Carre to be the sexiest of all the drinks in the classic New Orleans canon. Strong, stirred, and named after the Francophone term for the French Quarter, it's the kind of drink that seems ripe for a night of getting into trouble in alleyways around town. Invented in the 1930s by Walter Bergeron at the Hotel Monteleone, the cocktail's sultry finish and mysterious air feel kind of like sipping a little piece of New Orleans in a glass.

GLASSWARE: Rocks glass
GARNISH: Lemon twist

- ½ oz. Bénédictine

- ½ oz. rye whiskey

- ½ oz. Cognac

- ½ oz. sweet vermouth

- Dash of Peychaud's Bitters

- Dash of Angostura Bitters

1. Chill the rocks glass in the freezer.

2. Add all of the ingredients to the chilled glass, add ice, and stir until chilled.

3. Garnish with the lemon twist and enjoy.

CRAZY TOWN

With a name from a song frequently heard blaring from cover bands on Lower Broadway, this one's a riff on an Irish coffee that uses all local ingredients.

★

GLASSWARE: Collins glass
GARNISH: None

- **Cold-brew coffee, as needed**
- **1½ oz. Jack Daniel's Old No. 7 Tennessee Whiskey**
- **½ oz. honey**
- **½ oz. half-and-half**

1. Fill the Collins glass with ice and add cold-brew coffee until the glass is about three-fourths of the way full.
2. Place the remaining ingredients in a cocktail shaker, fill it two-thirds of the way with ice, and shake until chilled.
3. Strain the mixture over the cold-brew coffee and enjoy.

TENN

GATHER & SHARE

CINNAMON SUGAR BISCUITS | 9
Chocolate Gravy, Berries, Peanuts

DEVILED EGGS | 11
Garlic Chili Crisp, Chive

FRIED GREEN TOMATOES | 15
Whipped Feta, Bacon Jam

BISCUIT SITUATION

FRENCH TOAST | 16
Blueberry Compote, Buttermilk Syrup

FRIED CHICKEN | 18
Pimento Cheese, Hot Honey, Breakfast Potatoes

LOCAL BACON | 16
Scrambled Egg, White Cheddar, Tomato Jam,
Breakfast Potatoes

SOCK SAUSAGE GRAVY | 12
Black Pepper

FRIED GREEN TOMATOES | 15
Whipped Feta, Fig Jam, Arugula, Breakfast Potatoes

FISCHER'S SAUSAGE |
Over Easy Egg, Smoked Paprika Aioli

DOUBLE B
Pimento

RAMOS GIN FIZZ

NEW ORLEANS, LOUISIANA

Frothy, heady, and the ultimate tall, creamy, handsome sipper, the Ramos Gin Fizz is the quintessential New Orleans brunch drink.

★

GLASSWARE: Collins glass
GARNISH: Orange twist

- 2 oz. gin
- 1 oz. half-and-half
- ¾ oz. Simple Syrup (see page 20)
- ½ oz. fresh lemon juice
- ½ oz. fresh lime juice
- 2 dashes of orange blossom water
- 1 egg white
- Club soda, to top

1. Chill the Collins glass in the refrigerator.
2. Place all of the ingredients, except for the club soda, in a cocktail shaker and dry shake for 15 seconds.
3. Fill the shaker one-quarter of the way with ice and shake for 3 minutes.
4. Pour the cocktail into the chilled glass, top with club soda, garnish with the orange twist, and enjoy.

GRASSHOPPER

NEW ORLEANS, LOUISIANA

This minty, creamy after-dinner cocktail was created, according to legend, sometime in the 1920s by Philip Guichet of Tujague's. It took second prize in a 1928 New York drink competition, and has been a dessert-like favorite of drinkers with a sweet tooth ever since.

GLASSWARE: Cocktail glass
GARNISH: Fresh mint

- 1 oz. green crème de menthe
- 1 oz. white crème de cacao
- 1 oz. heavy cream

1. Chill the cocktail glass in the refrigerator.
2. Place all of the ingredients in a cocktail shaker, fill it two-thirds of the way with ice, and shake until chilled.
3. Strain into the chilled glass, garnish with fresh mint, and enjoy.

CADE'S COVE

HARRIET'S ROOFTOP
NASHVILLE, TENNESSEE

Harriet's Rooftop is a 21+ hot spot, perched atop the luxe 1 Hotel Nashville. Beverage manager Harrison Deakin leads the charge with lots of local-inspired sips, both boozy and spirit-free. The Cade's Cove marries beloved Tennessee whiskey with the sweet-and-sour punch of blackberry jam—at the bar, they source theirs from The Nashville Jam Company.

GLASSWARE: Rocks glass
GARNISH: Blackberries, fresh mint

- 1½ oz. Uncle Nearest 1856 Premium Aged Whiskey
- ¾ oz. fresh lemon juice
- ⅜ oz. Italicus Rosolio di Bergamotto
- ⅜ oz. blackberry jam
- 3 dashes of Peychaud's Bitters
- 5 fresh mint leaves
- 2 oz. ginger beer, to top

1. Place all of the ingredients, except for the ginger beer, in a cocktail shaker, fill it two-thirds of the way with ice, and shake until chilled.

2. Strain the cocktail over ice into the rocks glass and top with the ginger beer.

3. Garnish with blackberries and fresh mint and enjoy.

ROLLO RAIDERS

Yogurt—no, not the fruit-on-the-bottom kind—meets the icy, Nordic bite of aquavit and kümmel (a caraway and fennel–flavored liqueur) in this surprisingly tangy, creamy concoction.

GLASSWARE: Rocks glass
GARNISH: 2 strips of lemon peel, caraway seeds

- ¾ oz. plain full-fat yogurt
- ½ oz. Orgeat (see page 50)
- ¾ oz. fresh lemon juice

- ¾ oz. aquavit
- ¾ oz. kümmel
- ½ oz. gin (Beefeater preferred)

1. Place all of the ingredients in a cocktail shaker, fill it two-thirds of the way with ice, and shake until chilled.

2. Fill the rocks glass with crushed ice and double-strain the cocktail over it.

3. Garnish with the strips of lemon peel and caraway seeds and enjoy.

Q & A WITH
JEFF "BEACHBUM" BERRY

Mention the word "tiki," and one name automatically springs to most people's minds: Jeff "Beachbum" Berry. The country's foremost tiki scholar and co-owner of New Orleans's Latitude 29, Berry's charm and enthusiasm are infectious.

What inspired you to make the move to New Orleans and open Latitude 29?

Why New Orleans? That has a lot to do with the Tales of the Cocktail Awards. [My wife] Annene and I had never been to New Orleans before 2005, but we were looking for a place to move to from Los Angeles. There wasn't any city in the country that was doing it for us. Then we got invited to Tales [in 2005], stepped off the shuttle in the French Quarter, and it was like, "Where the hell has this place been all of our lives?" We felt like we weren't in the United States anymore, which was awesome.

Tiki demigod Donn Beach has long been rumored to be from New Orleans. What's the real story?

Up until very recently, I had heard that Donn Beach was born in New Orleans. So, moving here was like this full-circle thing. The guy who single-handedly invented the tiki bar and the tiki drink in 1934 was a New Orleanian, and we were bringing his drinks back. A lot of the drinks on our menu are Donn the Beachcomber drinks. Everybody stole from Donn, and he was sort of the big bang. But I've since found out from David Wondrich—the man who spoils everybody's favorite cocktail legends—that Donn was born in Mexia, Texas, but his parents were from New Orleans.

Close enough! In your mind, what does the ideal tiki bar look like?

At tiki bars you generally get two out of three things. The trifecta—good food, good drinks, and good atmosphere—is really hard to get. I always found that I would get two out of three at best. The Mai-Kai in Ft. Lauderdale was one of the few that delivered all three. What we really strived to do—with a much more limited budget and trying to use our imaginations—was to deliver on all those three accounts. I was pretty confident about the drinks, but it took [my wife] Annene working with our chef to really come up with food that paired well with the drinks.

Then, of course, for me the atmosphere was very important. You can't have a tiki bar without an immersive atmosphere. Otherwise, why even bother? I see a lot of places opening up, and they just look like your basic 1920s bar, but they're serving tiki food? Sorry, that's not good enough. You haven't committed yet.

MOLOKAI MISHAP

LATITUDE 29
NEW ORLEANS, LOUISIANA

In the Molokai Mishap, Cocchi Americano helps create a seaside-ready sipper perfect for an afternoon of beachy dreams.

★

GLASSWARE: Double rocks glass
GARNISH: None

- 1 oz. Cocchi Americano
- 1 oz. Rothman & Winter Orchard Peach
- 1 oz. pineapple juice

- 1 oz. rhum agricole
- 8 drops of Bittermens 'Elemakule Tiki Bitters

1. Place all of the ingredients in the double rocks glass and add 2 large ice cubes.

2. Stir until chilled and enjoy.

BRIDESMAID'S TEARS

ACME FEED & SEED
NASHVILLE, TENNESSEE

In case you've been living under a rock, Nashville is one of the country's most popular bachelorette party destinations. Therefore, it's no surprise to find plenty of cheeky pokes at last-minute bridal bashes on drink menus all over town. Here at Acme Feed & Seed's rooftop, Erica Stratton's sweet drink begins with Nashville's own Pickers Vodka.

GLASSWARE: Plastic cup
GARNISH: Lemon wedge

- 1½ oz. Pickers Pink Lemon Vodka
- ½ oz. Simple Syrup (see page 20)

- ¼ oz. black raspberry liqueur
- ¼ oz. fresh lemon juice
- Lemon-lime soda, to top

1. Fill the plastic cup with ice and build the cocktail in the glass, adding the ingredients in the order they are listed.

2. Gently stir, garnish with the lemon wedge, and enjoy.

L & N

ERGO
NASHVILLE, TENNESSEE

This cocktail is named after the Louisville and Nashville Railroad, which passed through Union Station from 1900 until 1979. The Union Station Nashville Yards Hotel's newly revamped flagship spot, ERGO, honors the 120-year history of its home with vibes and drinks like this one, inspired by the old-school romance of railway stations and eternal pull of adventure.

GLASSWARE: Coupe
GARNISH: Strip of orange peel

- 1½ oz. Cincoro Tequila Reposado
- ¾ oz. Honey & Basil Syrup (see recipe)
- 2 dashes of Angostura Bitters
- Bittermens Xocolatl Mole Bitters, to taste

1. Place all of the ingredients in a cocktail shaker, fill it two-thirds of the way with ice, and shake until chilled.

2. Strain the cocktail into the coupe, garnish with the strip of orange peel, and enjoy.

HONEY & BASIL SYRUP: Place 1 cup honey and 1 cup water in a saucepan and bring to a simmer, stirring until the honey has emulsified. Remove the pan from heat, add 2 handfuls of basil leaves, and let the mixture cool. Strain the syrup before using or storing in the refrigerator.

LITTLE BLACK STAR

EL LIBRE
NEW ORLEANS, LOUISIANA

Named after a song by local indie-rock band Hurray for the Riff Raff, this coffee-based concoction provides the necessary jolt of energy after a day walking through the heat of a New Orleans afternoon.

GLASSWARE: Coupe
GARNISH: Star anise pod

- 1½ oz. Brugal 1888 rum
- ½ oz. Coffee Syrup (see recipe)
- ½ oz. fresh lime juice
- ¼ oz. curaçao
- 1 bar spoon Luxardo maraschino liqueur

1. Chill the coupe in the freezer.
2. Place all of the ingredients in a cocktail shaker, fill it two-thirds of the way with ice, and shake until chilled.
3. Strain the cocktail into the coupe, garnish with the star anise, and enjoy.

COFFEE SYRUP: Place 1 cup water, 2¼ oz. brewed espresso, a dash of cinnamon, and a dash of chili powder in a saucepan and bring the mixture to a boil, stirring occasionally. Add 2 cups sugar and stir until it has dissolved. Remove the pan from heat and let the mixture cool completely. Strain the syrup through a fine-mesh sieve before using or storing in the refrigerator.

DRINK OF LAUGHTER AND FORGETTING

CURE
NEW ORLEANS, LOUISIANA

A Crescent City classic that dances between bitter and herbal with ingenious dexterity, thanks to the interplay between the Green Chartreuse and Cynar.

GLASSWARE: Cocktail glass
GARNISH: 14 drops of Angostura Bitters

- 1½ oz. Cynar
- ½ oz. Green Chartreuse
- ¾ oz. fresh lime juice

- ½ oz. Demerara Syrup (see page 63)

1. Place all of the ingredients in a cocktail shaker, fill it two-thirds of the way with ice, and shake until chilled.

2. Strain into the cocktail glass, garnish with the bitters, and enjoy.

MAGIC TREE

CURE
NEW ORLEANS, LOUISIANA

Mastiha, a Greek liqueur made from the aromatic resin of the hyper-rare mastic tree, isn't an ingredient you're likely find on a grocery store shelf. With a noticeable sweetness and notes of clove, however, it is one you'll find yourself returning to time and again after making this cocktail, which balances out the spirit's piney notes with a swish of lime and the cooling embrace of cucumber.

GLASSWARE: Coupe
GARNISH: 7 drops of The Bitter Truth Cucumber Bitters

- 2 slices of cucumber
- 1½ oz. Stoupakis Homeric Chios Mastiha Liqueur
- ½ oz. Suze
- ½ oz. navy-strength gin (Royal Dock preferred)
- ¾ oz. fresh lime juice
- ¼ oz. Simple Syrup (see page 20)

1. Place the cucumber in a cocktail shaker and muddle.

2. Add ice and the remaining ingredients and shake until chilled.

3. Double-strain the cocktail into the coupe, garnish with the bitters, and enjoy.

QUARTER TANK OF GASOLINE

BLACK RABBIT
NASHVILLE, TENNESSEE

This cocktail was born when Tommy Hartzog, Black Rabbit's managing partner, wanted to feature a drink that reminded him of the sassafras tea his father would sip in his rocking chair on the front porch—that was his father's way of winding down after a long day working in the yard in Mt. Juliet, Tennessee. The result is this light and refreshing take on a Whiskey Smash.

GLASSWARE: Rocks glass
GARNISH: Fresh mint

- **2 oz. Nelson's Green Brier Tennessee Whiskey**
- **1 oz. Sassafras Syrup (see recipe)**
- **½ oz. fresh lemon juice**

1. Place all of the ingredients in a cocktail shaker, fill it two-thirds of the way with ice, and shake until chilled.

2. Strain the cocktail over ice into the rocks glass, garnish with fresh mint, and enjoy.

SASSAFRAS SYRUP: Place 3 sprigs of fresh mint, the zest of 2 lemons, and 1½ cups Simple Syrup (see page 20) in a large mason jar and muddle. Add 1½ cups sassafras tea concentrate, shake to combine, and chill the syrup in the refrigerator overnight before using.

FJORDIAN SLIP

THREE MUSES
NEW ORLEANS, LOUISIANA

The use of birch liqueur—distilled with birch bark harvested from the forests of Iceland—adds a woodsy, earthy depth to the cocktail's sweetness, keeping it from tipping over into treacly territory.

GLASSWARE: Coupe
GARNISH: Lemon wheel

- 1½ oz. unaged rum
- ¾ oz. Foss Björk birch liqueur
- ½ oz. Honey Syrup (see page 73)
- ½ oz. fresh lemon juice

1. Place all of the ingredients in a cocktail shaker, fill it two-thirds of the way with ice, and shake until chilled.

2. Double-strain into the coupe, garnish with the lemon wheel, and enjoy.

NERTZ!

Tangipahoa Parish is best known for their prolific production of oranges. This cocktail taps this agricultural heritage, and then runs in an astonishing number of directions.

GLASSWARE: Coupe

GARNISH: Strip of orange peel

- 1½ oz. cachaça
- ¾ oz. pineapple juice
- ½ oz. fresh lemon juice

- ½ oz. grenadine
- 2 dashes of orange bitters
- Dash of Angostura Bitters

1. Chill the coupe in the freezer.

2. Place all of the ingredients in a cocktail shaker, fill it two-thirds of the way with ice, and shake until chilled.

3. Double-strain the cocktail into the chilled coupe, express the strip of orange peel over the cocktail, use it as a garnish, and enjoy.

NO TRUE SCOTSMAN

SINATRA BAR & LOUNGE
NASHVILLE, TENNESSEE

Crisp and fresh, The Botanist's Islay gin is one for connoisseurs to start paying attention to.

★

GLASSWARE: Rocks glass

GARNISH: Cocktail onions

- 2 oz. The Botanist Islay Dry Gin
- 1 oz. Lo-Fi Dry Vermouth
- ¼ oz. olive brine
- 2 dashes of Berg & Hauck's Original Celery Bitters

1. Place all of the ingredients in a cocktail shaker, fill it two-thirds of the way with ice, and shake until chilled.

2. Strain the cocktail over ice into the rocks glass, garnish with cocktail onions, and enjoy.

GUNSHOP FIZZ

CURE
NEW ORLEANS, LOUISIANA

"While utilizing bitters as a base spirit is not a new idea, it is something that one rarely sees in contemporary recipes," Cure's Kirk Estopinal says of the Gunshop Fizz, which draws inspiration from the classic Angostura Fizz. Just to kick the bitter factor up another notch (because, why not?), the recipe calls for a final flourish of Sanbittèr, a fire engine–red Italian bitter soda.

GLASSWARE: Collins glass
GARNISH: Cucumber wheel

- 2 oz. Peychaud's Bitters
- 1 oz. fresh lemon juice
- 1 oz. Simple Syrup (see page 20)
- 2 strawberries, hulled
- 3 cucumber slices
- 3 strips of grapefruit peel
- 3 strips of orange peel
- San Pellegrino Sanbittèr, to top

1. Place all of the ingredients, except for the Sanbitter, in a cocktail shaker and muddle until well combined. Let the mixture steep for 2 minutes.
2. Add ice and shake until chilled.
3. Strain over ice into the Collins glass and top with the Sanbitter.
4. Garnish with the cucumber wheel and enjoy.

OFFICIAL DRINK OF NASHVILLE

L.A. JACKSON
NASHVILLE, TENNESSEE

A creation from the popular Gulch rooftop spot L.A. Jackson, this was crowned the "Official Drink of Nashville" at the 2018 Music City Food and Wine Festival. Originally dubbed "The 615," this cocktail features some of Tennessee's greatest local offerings.

GLASSWARE: Collins glass
GARNISH: Fresh mint, bee pollen

- 1½ oz. Chattanooga 1816 Reserve Whiskey
- ¾ oz. pineapple juice
- ½ oz. fresh lemon juice
- ½ oz. Aperol
- ¼ oz. curaçao
- ¼ oz. honey
- ¼ oz. Ginger Syrup (see page 129)
- 2 dashes of Angostura Bitters

1. Place all of the ingredients in a cocktail shaker, fill it two-thirds of the way with ice, and shake until chilled.

2. Pour the cocktail into the Collins glass and fill the glass with crushed ice.

3. Garnish with fresh mint and bee pollen and enjoy.

KING CAKE MILKSHAKE

THE COMPANY BURGER
NEW ORLEANS, LOUISIANA

King cakes rule Mardi Gras season (and rightfully so), but it's easy to get burnt out trying to properly pair your king cake du jour with the right boozy chaser. This liquored-up milkshake is, perhaps, the best of both luscious worlds.

GLASSWARE: Sundae glass
GARNISH: Dusting of cinnamon

- ½ oz. **Tempus Fugit Crème de Cacao**

- ½ oz. **Amaro CioCiaro**

- ½ oz. **Fireball whisky**

- ½ oz. **Galliano**

- 2 dashes of **Fee Brothers Old Fashioned Bitters**

- ½ teaspoon **cinnamon**

- 12 oz. **vanilla ice cream**

- 2 oz. **whole milk**

1. Place all of the ingredients, except for the ice cream and milk, a cocktail shaker and chill in the refrigerator for 30 minutes.

2. Chill the sundae glass in the refrigerator.

3. Place the ice cream, milk, and chilled mixture in a blender and pulse until smooth.

4. Pour the cocktail into the chilled sundae glass, garnish with the dusting of cinnamon, swirl the cinnamon with a straw, and enjoy.

CLASSIC HURRICANE

NEW ORLEANS, LOUISIANA

Okay, sure, go ahead and try the sugared-up, ruby-colored one that Pat O'Brien's has made famous. It's fun. But then make yourself a real-deal Hurricane, and taste just how nuanced—and refreshing—the drink can be. I promise you'll never go back.

GLASSWARE: Hurricane glass
GARNISH: Orange wheel

- 2 oz. light rum
- 2 oz. dark rum
- 1 oz. fresh lime juice
- 2 oz. passion fruit juice
- ½ oz. Simple Syrup (see page 20)
- ½ oz. orange juice
- ½ oz. grenadine

1. Place all of the ingredients in a cocktail shaker, fill it two-thirds of the way with ice, and shake until chilled.

2. Fill the Hurricane glass one-quarter of the way with crushed ice and strain the cocktail over it.

3. Garnish with the orange wheel and enjoy.

STRANGE BREW

HUSK
NASHVILLE, TENNESSEE

Husk Nashville's cocktail program, led by Adam Morgan, focuses on using homegrown ingredients and by-products from its outstanding culinary program. Not veering from the restaurant's dedication to all things local, Adam's take on the omnipresent Espresso Martini is a caffeinated crowd-pleaser, using local darling Crema coffee alongside sherry and tequila.

GLASSWARE: Nick & Nora glass
GARNISH: Freshly grated nutmeg

- 1 oz. tequila
- 1 oz. Mr Black Coffee Amaro
- 1 oz. chilled coffee
- ½ oz. Coffee Cordial (see recipe)
- ¼ oz. oloroso sherry
- Pinch of salt
- Dash of Angostura Bitters

1. Place all of the ingredients in a cocktail shaker, fill it two-thirds of the way with ice, and shake until chilled.

2. Strain the cocktail into the Nick & Nora glass, garnish with nutmeg, and enjoy.

COFFEE CORDIAL: Combine equal parts sugar and hot coffee, add ½ oz. vanilla liqueur, and stir to combine. Let the cordial cool completely before using or storing.

MIDWEST

Aloe? It's Me ★ Morelos Sour
Cherry Blossom ★ Mr. Smooth
Postcards from Palawan
Vinegar? I Barely Know Her!
Bonapera ★ Dunbar's Numbers
Camera Obscura ★ Hot Rush
Acapulco ★ Miniskirt
Polar Vortex ★ Anne with an E
Lone Wolf Sour ★ Cold-Peated Old Fashioned
Parallelogram ★ Bonecrusher
Oliveto ★ Floridita #3 ★ Gimlet

After some time lounging in New Orleans and Nashville, it is tempting to give up our cross-country dreams and remain where the weather is warm, the sun bright, and the cocktail hours exceptional. But soldier on we must, and when you hear about our next stops, you're sure to get a little pep in your step—we're headed to the Midwest. While there, we'll hit Chicago, a town that is, by every meaningful metric, one of the world's great cities. That's especially the case in terms of cocktails. Whether you are there in the summer and looking for something that will allow you to ease into that months-long celebration, or visiting in the winter and looking for a serve that can remove the chill from your bones, these bars and cocktails are a terrific place to start.

Chicago may be the region's capital, but the Twin Cities, Minneapolis and St. Paul, Minnesota, stand shoulder to shoulder with the Windy City when it comes to mixology. In fact, the scene there can stand beside any of the other locations in the book. Skeptical? Just cast a quick glance at the Hot Rush (see page 230) and the Anne with an E on page 237—they are some of the best-looking and best-crafted drinks in the entire book.

ALOE? IT'S ME

ABA
CHICAGO, ILLINOIS

As one of the most popular cocktails at Aba since the first location opened in Chicago's Fulton Market neighborhood in 2018, the Aloe? It's Me appeals to each guest for different reasons, with complex tasting notes that are the product of a layered and carefully curated recipe. It's also the ideal introduction to mezcal.

GLASSWARE: Double rocks glass
GARNISH: Fresh parsley, Aleppo pepper

- ¾ oz. fresh lime juice
- 1 oz. preferred green juice
- ½ oz. Honey Syrup (see page 73)

- ½ oz. Chareau Aloe Liqueur
- 1½ oz. Jalapeño Mezcal (see recipe)

1. Place all of the ingredients in a cocktail shaker and dry shake for 15 seconds.

2. Fill the double rocks glass with ice and pour the cocktail over it.

3. Garnish with fresh parsley and Aleppo pepper and enjoy.

JALAPEÑO MEZCAL: Place 1 halved jalapeño pepper in a 750 ml bottle of mezcal and let the mixture steep for 24 hours. Strain before using or storing.

MORELOS SOUR

CENTRO
MINNEAPOLIS, MINNESOTA

The perfect combination of mellow heat, a touch of sweet, a little earthiness, and a puckery-sour flavor makes this an expertly balanced cocktail.

GLASSWARE: Rocks glass
GARNISH: Tajín-dusted orange wedge

- Sal de gusano, for the rim

- ¾ oz. Simple Syrup (see page 20)

- 2 oz. bourbon

- ½ oz. fresh lemon juice

- ¾ oz. chipotle sour

1. Wet the rim of the rocks glass and coat it with sal de gusano.

2. Place the remaining ingredients in a cocktail shaker, fill it two-thirds of the way with ice, and shake until chilled.

3. Pour the contents of the shaker into the rimmed glass, garnish with the orange wedge, and enjoy.

CHERRY BLOSSOM

BAMBOLA
CHICAGO, ILLINOIS

The Plum Paint should not break away from the glass when you strain the cocktail into it. If it does, the paint was made incorrectly. Instead, you want it to slowly leach into the glass, turning the cocktail a light pink as you consume it.

GLASSWARE: Coupe
GARNISH: Plum Paint (see recipe)

- 1¼ oz. shochu
- ¾ oz. Roku Japanese Gin
- ¼ oz. white crème de cacao
- ½ oz. Cherry Blossom Syrup (see recipe)
- ¾ oz. fresh lemon juice

1. Chill the coupe in the freezer.
2. Place all of the ingredients in a cocktail shaker, fill it two-thirds of the way with ice, and shake until chilled.
3. Brush the bowl of the chilled coupe with the Plum Paint, double-strain the cocktail into the coupe, and enjoy.

CHERRY BLOSSOM SYRUP: Place 200 grams cherry blossom paste, 500 grams sugar, and 500 grams water in a blender and puree until combined. Use immediately or store in the refrigerator.

PLUM PAINT: Place 100 grams dried plum powder and 10 oz. water in a blender and puree on high until smooth. Use immediately or store in the refrigerator for up to 1 week.

MR. SMOOTH

DAKOTA
MINNEAPOLIS, MINNESOTA

The Mr. Smooth was named for Irv Williams, an American jazz legend and lifelong Twin Cities resident, and was designed to capture the complexity and strength of its legendary namesake. This is the version that Irv himself approved before his passing at 100 years of age.

GLASSWARE: Coupe
GARNISH: Strip of orange peel

- 2 oz. bourbon
- ¼ oz. Cognac
- ¼ oz. Cynar
- ¼ oz. Demerara Syrup (see page 63)
- 2 dashes of Angostura Bitters

1. Place all of the ingredients in a mixing glass, fill it two-thirds of the way with ice, and stir until chilled.

2. Strain the cocktail into the coupe, garnish with the strip of orange peel, and enjoy.

POSTCARDS FROM PALAWAN

HAI HAI
MINNEAPOLIS, MINNESOTA

A play on a spicy Margarita, this drink uses real tamarind for an earthy, tart flavor, plus pineapple to balance its acidity and spice from the Thai chile.

★

GLASSWARE: Rocks glass
GARNISH: Thin pineapple slice, pineapple leaves

- 2 oz. Tamarind & Thai Chile Mezcal (see recipe)
- ¾ oz. Simple Syrup (see page 20)
- 1 oz. pineapple juice
- ¾ oz. fresh lime juice

1. Place all of the ingredients in a cocktail shaker, fill it two-thirds of the way with ice, and shake until chilled.

2. Strain the cocktail over ice into the rocks glass, garnish with the slice of pineapple and pineapple leaves, and enjoy.

TAMARIND & THAI CHILE MEZCAL: Combine 1 (750 ml) bottle of La Luna Mezcal with 4 chopped Thai chiles, ½ pineapple, rind removed and chopped, and 6 tamarind pods, shells removed. Let the mixture steep for 24 to 48 hours. Strain before using or storing.

VINEGAR? I BARELY KNOW HER!

THE BERKSHIRE ROOM
CHICAGO, ILLINOIS

America's favorite homegrown vodka—Tito's, which is made in Austin, Texas—forms the foundation of this refresher.

★

GLASSWARE: Collins glass
GARNISH: Fresh Thai basil

- 1½ oz. Tito's Vodka
- ¼ oz. St. George Aqua Perfecta Basil Eau de Vie
- ⅛ oz. Capirete 20 Year Sherry Vinegar
- ½ oz. fresh lemon juice
- ½ oz. Strawberry Syrup (see recipe)
- 1½ oz. Fever-Tree Indian Tonic

1. Place all of the ingredients, except for the tonic, in a cocktail shaker, fill it two-thirds of the way with ice, and give the cocktail a short, hard shake.

2. Pour the tonic into the cocktail shaker. Fill the Collins glass with pebble ice and strain the cocktail over it.

3. Garnish with fresh Thai basil and enjoy.

STRAWBERRY SYRUP: Place 1½ cups chopped strawberries in a saucepan and cook over low heat until they are soft. Muddle the cooked strawberries, add 1 cup sugar and 1 cup water, and bring to a boil. Remove the pan from heat, cover the pan, and let the mixture steep for 15 minutes. After 15 minutes, place the pan in an ice bath until the mixture is cool. Strain the syrup before using or storing in the refrigerator.

BONAPERA

MARTINA
MINNEAPOLIS, MINNESOTA

Typical of the drinks and food at Martina, the Bonapera layers complex flavor elements into something that ends up feeling seamless, smooth, and elemental.

GLASSWARE: Tumbler

GARNISH: None

- ½ oz. brandy & grappa blend
- ⅗ oz. Cocchi Rosa Americano
- ½ oz. iced yerba maté tea
- ⅒ oz. rye whiskey
- ⅒ oz. St. George Spiced Pear Liqueur
- ⅒ oz. Demerara Syrup (see page 63)
- 2 dashes of Angostura Bitters

1. Place all of the ingredients in a mixing glass, fill it two-thirds of the way with ice, and stir until chilled.

2. Strain the cocktail over ice into the tumbler and enjoy.

DUNBAR'S NUMBERS

P.S. STEAK
MINNEAPOLIS, MINNESOTA

This recipe can also be scaled up as a punch for parties—just omit the shaking and add sparkling sake right before guests arrive.

GLASSWARE: Punch cup

GARNISH: None

- ½ oz. fresh citrus
- ⁷⁄₁₀ oz. lychee liqueur
- ⁷⁄₁₀ oz. blanc vermouth
- 1 oz. vodka
- 1½ oz. bitter orange liqueur
- 4 oz. iced hibiscus tea
- 1 oz. sparkling sake

1. Place all of the ingredients, except for the sparkling sake, in a cocktail shaker, fill it two-thirds of the way with ice, and shake until chilled.

2. Add the sparkling sake, strain the cocktail over 1 large ice cube into the punch cup, and enjoy.

CAMERA OBSCURA

BOKEH
CHICAGO, ILLINOIS

According to Rick Weber, Bokeh's owner: "This was one of those random conversation–inspired cocktails. We were talking about Branson, Missouri, and one of our bartenders had never been there, which somehow devolved into a discussion about Gallagher—the comedian who used to smash watermelons in his comedy routine—and I decided to make a watermelon juice–inspired cocktail in his honor."

GLASSWARE: Collins glass
GARNISH: Fresh mint, lemon twist

- 2 oz. Mint Bourbon (see recipe)
- 2 oz. Watermelon Juice (see recipe)
- 1 oz. fresh lemon juice
- 1 oz. Honey Syrup (see page 73)
- 3 dashes of Peychaud's Bitters

1. Place all of the ingredients in a cocktail shaker, fill it two-thirds of the way with ice, and shake until chilled.

2. Strain the cocktail over ice into the Collins glass, garnish with fresh mint and the lemon twist, and enjoy.

MINT BOURBON: Place 1 liter of bourbon and 2 large handfuls of fresh mint in a large container and steep for 24 hours. Strain before using or storing.

WATERMELON JUICE: Puree watermelon chunks in a blender, strain through a fine-mesh sieve, and use immediately or store in the refrigerator.

HOT RUSH

SIDEBAR AT SURDYK'S
MINNEAPOLIS, MINNESOTA

"At Sidebar, we incorporate many ingredients stocked in our liquor store and cheese shop," says co-owner Taylor Surdyk. "Not only does it create a nice synergy, it also gives us the opportunity to show guests creative ways to use the products we sell. The Hot Rush uses Cry Baby Craig's Hot Honey, a local product that brings the heat—which is welcome on a cold Minnesota day."

GLASSWARE: Double rocks glass
GARNISH: Silgochu

- 1½ oz. Buffalo Trace Bourbon
- ¾ oz. fresh Meyer lemon juice
- ¾ oz. Cry Baby Craig's Hot Honey

1. Place all of the ingredients in a mixing glass, fill it two-thirds of the way with ice, and stir until chilled.

2. Strain over 1 large ice cube into the double rocks glass, garnish with silgochu, and enjoy.

ACAPULCO

BASEMENT BAR AT SOOKI & MIMI
MINNEAPOLIS, MINNESOTA

Accessible in the alley behind Sooki & Mimi in Uptown and located beneath the restaurant, the Basement Bar is modeled after just that—your grandparents' basement. Low ceilings, comfortable couches and seats with retro patterns, a vintage turntable and reel-to-reel tape deck, and 1970s décor transport drinkers to an earlier era. Tacos provide sustenance, while the cocktail menu includes a dose of nostalgia. Just like grandma and grandpa's house, you won't want to leave.

This version of the classic tiki drink is big on flavor without leaning too heavily on sweetness. It's nostalgic and modern, all in one glass. For the rum, choose Appleton Estate, Hamilton, or Smith & Cross.

GLASSWARE: Coupe
GARNISH: Pineapple leaf

- **2 oz. fresh pineapple juice**
- **1 oz. reposado tequila**
- **1 oz. Jamaican rum**

- **1 oz. fresh grapefruit juice**
- **Dash of Green Tabasco, or to taste**

1. Place all of the ingredients in a cocktail shaker, fill it two-thirds of the way with ice, and shake until chilled.

2. Strain into the coupe, garnish with the pineapple leaf, and enjoy.

MINISKIRT

BYRDHOUSE
CHICAGO, ILLINOIS

Pisco's aromatic, floral, and herbaceous qualities work wonders with the other ingredients in this inventive serve.

★

GLASSWARE: Coupe
GARNISH: Maraschino cherry

- ½ oz. Macchu Pisco
- ½ oz. Chinola Passion Fruit Liqueur
- ½ oz. Cocchi Americano
- ½ oz. Aperol
- ½ oz. fresh lemon juice
- Strip of lemon peel

1. Chill the coupe in the freezer.

2. Place all of the ingredients, except for the strip of lemon peel, in a cocktail shaker, fill it two-thirds of the way with ice, and shake until chilled.

3. Strain the cocktail into the chilled coupe and express the lemon peel over the top.

4. Garnish with the cherry and enjoy.

POLAR VORTEX

ELIXIR LOUNGE
CHICAGO, ILLINOIS

Named for the infamous effect that is caused by Lake Michigan and responsible for Chicago's unique weather.

★

GLASSWARE: Collins glass
GARNISH: Sugar-coated blueberries

- 2 oz. Blueberry Tea–Infused Vodka (see recipe)
- ½ oz. Lavender Syrup (see page 109)

- Cream soda, to top
- 1 oz. cream of coconut

1. Fill the Collins glass with ice, add the vodka and syrup, and stir until chilled.

2. Top with cream soda and layer the cream of coconut on top of the cocktail.

3. Garnish with sugar-coated blueberries and enjoy.

BLUEBERRY TEA–INFUSED VODKA: Place 2 bags of blueberry tea and a 750 ml bottle of vodka in a large mason jar and steep for 4 hours. Remove the tea bags and use immediately or store.

ANNE WITH AN E

EMERALD LOUNGE
ST. PAUL, MINNESOTA

Tart, dry, and austere, with a silky-smooth texture and an herbaceous nose.

★

GLASSWARE: Coupe
GARNISH: Spritz of Green Chartreuse, edible flower petal

- **2 oz. London dry gin**
- **¾ oz. fresh lemon juice**
- **½ oz. curaçao**
- **½ oz. Honey Syrup (see page 73)**
- **¾ oz. egg white**
- **2 drops of 10 Percent Saline Solution (see page 313)**
- **Large strip of grapefruit peel**

1. Chill the coupe in the freezer.
2. Place all of the ingredients in a cocktail shaker and dry shake for 15 seconds.
3. Add ice and shake until chilled.
4. Double-strain the cocktail into the chilled coupe, spritz it with the Green Chartreuse, garnish with the edible flower petal, and enjoy.

LONE WOLF SOUR

LONE WOLF
CHICAGO, ILLINOIS

Lone Wolf is a high-volume cocktail and beer bar in the heart of Chicago's West Loop. They pride themselves on their whiskey selection and ability to make drinks fast without sacrificing quality, as you'll see when you whip up one of these.

GLASSWARE: Rocks glass
GARNISH: Strip of lemon peel

- 2 oz. Maker's Mark
- ¾ oz. fresh lemon juice
- ¾ oz. Mango & Passion Fruit Syrup (see recipe)
- 2 dashes of Angostura Bitters

1. Place all of the ingredients in a cocktail shaker, fill it two-thirds of the way with ice, and shake until chilled.

2. Strain the cocktail over ice into the rocks glass, express the strip of lemon peel over it, garnish the drink with the lemon peel, and enjoy.

MANGO & PASSION FRUIT SYRUP: Place 2 parts mango puree and 1 part passion fruit puree in a mason jar and stir to combine. Add an equal amount of Simple Syrup (see page 20) and use immediately or store in the refrigerator.

COLD-PEATED
OLD FASHIONED

BROTHER JUSTUS WHISKEY COMPANY
MINNEAPOLIS, MINNESOTA

Brother Justus's cold-peated whiskey shines in this classic cocktail. Using the only cold-peated method in the world—dubbed the Aitkin County Process—means that the herbaceous flavors of Minnesota peat complement the smoky notes, instead of being overpowered by them.

GLASSWARE: Rocks glass
GARNISH: Strip of orange peel

- **2 oz. Brother Justus Cold-Peated Whiskey**

- **½ oz. Simple Syrup (see page 20)**

- **2 dashes of Angostura Bitters**

1. Place all of the ingredients in a mixing glass and stir until thoroughly combined.

2. Add 1 large ice cube to the rocks glass, pour the cocktail into the glass, and gently stir.

3. Express the strip of orange peel over the cocktail, use it as a garnish, and enjoy.

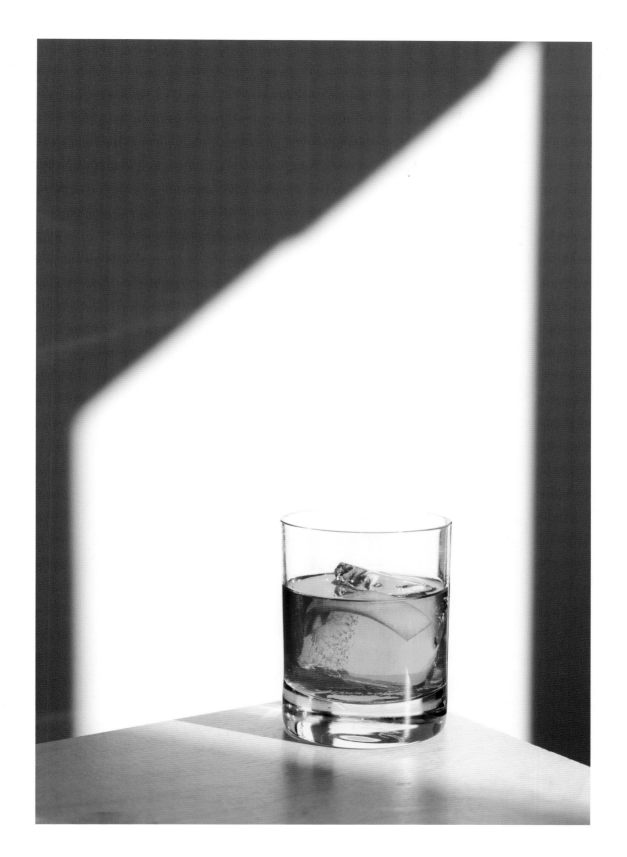

PARALLELOGRAM

LONG ROOM
CHICAGO, ILLINOIS

This cocktail's name is a throwback to the creator, Long Room bartender Ryan Rezvani, spending 14 years as a teacher. It also works incredibly well as either a winter sipper or a summer porch pounder—depending on your mood!

GLASSWARE: Nick & Nora glass
GARNISH: Lime wheel

- **Guerrero rub, for the rim**
- **1½ oz. silver tequila**
- **¾ oz. Aperol**
- **¾ oz. fresh lime juice**
- **¼ oz. agave nectar**
- **3 dashes of Bitter Ex Aromatic Bitters**
- **6 dashes of Bitter Ex Hot Pepper Bitters**

1. Wet the rim of the Nick & Nora glass and rim it with the rub.

2. Place the tequila, Aperol, lime juice, and agave nectar in a cocktail shaker, fill it two-thirds of the way with ice, and shake until chilled.

3. Strain the cocktail into the rimmed glass and top with the bitters.

4. Garnish with the lime wheel and enjoy.

BONECRUSHER

TATTERSALL DISTILLING
MINNEAPOLIS, MINNESOTA

Simply put, there is no substitute for Tatersall's Toasted Coconut Aquavit here. If you are intrigued by this serve—and believe me, you should be—it is worth taking any measures necessary to source a bottle.

GLASSWARE: Tumbler

GARNISH: Lime wheel

- **2 oz. Tattersall Toasted Coconut Aquavit**
- **¾ oz. pineapple juice**
- **¾ oz. Matcha Syrup (see recipe)**
- **½ oz. fresh lime juice**

1. Place all of the ingredients in a cocktail shaker, fill it two-thirds of the way with ice, and shake until chilled.

2. Strain the cocktail over 1 large ice cube into the tumbler, garnish with the lime wheel, and enjoy.

MATCHA SYRUP: In a saucepan, combine 1 cup water, 1 cup sugar, and 1 teaspoon matcha tea powder. Bring the mixture to a simmer, stirring to dissolve the sugar and powder. Remove the pan from heat and let the syrup cool completely. Strain before using or storing in the refrigerator.

OLIVETO

This was the most popular drink at the now-closed Marvel Bar.

GLASSWARE: Stemless wineglass
GARNISH: None

- 2 oz. London dry gin
- ⅘ oz. fresh lemon juice
- ⅖ oz. Rich Simple Syrup (see recipe)
- ⅖ oz. Licor 43
- ½ oz. extra-virgin olive oil
- 1 egg white

1. Place all of the ingredients in a cocktail shaker, add 3 ice cubes, and shake until the ice has almost completely dissolved.

2. Strain the cocktail into the stemless wineglass and enjoy.

RICH SIMPLE SYRUP: Place 2 cups sugar and 1 cup water in a saucepan and bring it to a boil, stirring to dissolve the sugar. Remove the pan from heat and let the syrup cool completely before using or storing.

FLORIDITA #3

The best elements of the two rums are brought out beautifully by the Luxardo, which in cocktail making functions similarly to the way that salt does in cooking.

GLASSWARE: Goblet
GARNISH: Cherry, lime wheel

- 1 oz. Plantation 3 Stars Rum
- ¾ oz. Flor de Caña 4 Year White Rum
- ¼ oz. Luxardo maraschino liqueur
- ¾ oz. fresh lime juice
- ½ oz. grapefruit juice
- 1 (heaping) teaspoon caster (superfine) sugar

1. Place all of the ingredients in a cocktail shaker, add 1 cup crushed ice, and flash mix with a hand blender.

2. Pour the contents of the shaker into the goblet, garnish with the cherry and lime wheel, and enjoy.

GIMLET

A precisely made, balanced, and complex version of the classic cocktail.

★

GLASSWARE: Nick & Nora glass
GARNISH: Dehydrated lime wheel

- 1 oz. Fords Gin
- ½ oz. Old Duff Genever
- ¼ oz. Lustau Amontillado Los Arcos Sherry
- ¾ oz. fresh lime juice
- ¾ oz. Mixed Citrus Oleo (see recipe)
- Dash of Angostura Bitters

1. Chill the Nick & Nora glass in the freezer.
2. Place all of the ingredients in a cocktail shaker, fill it two-thirds of the way with ice, and shake until chilled.
3. Strain into the chilled Nick & Nora glass, garnish with the dehydrated lime wheel, and enjoy.

MIXED CITRUS OLEO: Combine mixed citrus scraps (the ends, peels, or husks after juicing from citrus fruits like oranges, lemons, and grapefruits) with an equal amount of sugar (by weight) in a vacuum bag. Let the mixture macerate in the refrigerator for 24 to 36 hours, massaging it occasionally to dissolve the sugar. Strain the oleo through a mesh tea strainer before using or storing in the refrigerator.

SOUTHWEST

CHILTON ★ FROZEN MARGARITA

RANCH WATER ★ LANDRACE

THE LITTLEJOHN COBBLER

JOHNNY'S BOILERMAKER SHOT

ROSEWATER SOUR ★ THE HATCHBACK

TARRAGUEUR ★ THE NOMAD

TEXAS GENTLEMAN

THE GREENEVILLE GRANNY

BERTA'S CUP ★ OLD TIMER

EL PAJARO

Having made the most of our time in the heartland, and reminded ourselves that it is far more than the "flyover country" that some ignorantly brand it as, it is time to move on to another area that is polarizing across the country: Texas. Texas is a tough place to get a firm grip on, as what holds in one part of the Lone Star State is unthinkable in another. This resistance to encapsulation is summed up beautifully by one of America's greatest authors, John Steinbeck, who said "I have said that Texas is a state of mind, but I think it is more than that. It is a mystique closely approximating a religion. And this is true to the extent that people either passionately love Texas or passionately hate it and, as in other religions, few people dare to inspect it for fear of losing their bearings in mystery or paradox. But I think there will be little quarrel with my feeling that Texas is one thing. For all its enormous range of space, climate, and physical appearance, and for all the internal squabbles, contentions, and strivings, Texas has a tight cohesiveness perhaps stronger than any other section of America. Rich, poor, Panhandle, Gulf, city, country, Texas is the obsession, the proper study, and the passionate possession of all Texans."

The love Texans have for their state is undeniable, and they continually search for new methods that allow them to maintain that ardor in spite of its extremity. Case in point, to deal with the excessive heat that reigns for much of the year, they've developed a strong tradition of refreshers like the Ranch Water (see page 260), Chilton (see page 256), and Frozen Margarita (see page 259). Add to that the continually shifting demographics and a statewide distilling boom, and the bars in Texas can proudly stand beside any in this book in terms of quality and creativity—not that they wouldn't even if those two characteristics were entirely absent.

CHILTON

The Chilton is one of the two "classic" cocktails that can be attributed to Texas. According to members of the Lubbock Country Club, a local doctor, Dr. Chilton to be exact, asked his bartender to mix the juice of two lemons with vodka and soda and serve it over ice, with a salt rim. Ta-da! The Chilton was born! It's a sunny and arid day on the Panhandle in a glass. That's one thing about these West Texas cocktails...they're always as dry as the land they hail from.

GLASSWARE: Collins glass
GARNISH: Lemon wheel

- Salt, for the rim
- 1½ oz. Texas vodka (Dripping Springs or Cinco preferred)
- Juice of 2 lemons
- Topo Chico, to top

1. Wet the rim of the Collins glass and coat it with salt.
2. Fill the glass with ice, add the vodka and lemon juice, and top with Topo Chico.
3. Gently stir the cocktail, garnish with the lemon wheel, and enjoy.

FROZEN MARGARITA

DALLAS, TEXAS

In 1971, Mariano Martinez had a problem. Too many people wanted Margaritas and it was taking too long to make them. After a sleepless night, Mariano stopped by a convenience store on the way to work for coffee, saw a slushy machine, and the rest is history. Soon, he was making Margaritas in a soft-serve ice cream machine, and he called it "The World's First Frozen Margarita Machine." Over time, the Frozen Margarita has undoubtedly become the most popular cocktail in the entire state of Texas.

GLASSWARE: Mug or Margarita coupe
GARNISH: Lime wedge

- **2 oz. silver tequila**
- **1 oz. fresh lime juice**
- **¾ oz. Cointreau**

1. Chill the glass in the freezer.

2. Place all of the ingredients and 1 cup ice in a blender and puree until smooth.

3. Pour the cocktail into the chilled glass, garnish with the lime wedge, and enjoy.

RANCH WATER

This is, absolutely, the most important of all Texas cocktails. Nowadays, there are as many versions of the Ranch Water's origin story as there are cans claiming to be "Ranch Water" being sold at a convenience store. But don't buy any of that garbage. You're better than that. Follow these simple directions when you need the refreshment that only the Ranch Water can supply.

GLASSWARE: Topo Chico bottle

GARNISH: Lime wedge

- **1 (12 oz.) bottle of Topo Chico**
- **1½ oz. tequila**
- **¼ oz. fresh lime juice**

1. Pour out 2 oz. of the Topo Chico and add the tequila and lime juice to the bottle.

2. Garnish with the lime wedge and enjoy.

LANDRACE

Okay, so…here's a little secret…there's a speakeasy inside a cocktail bar in San Antonio. Strange, yes. But the Downstairs at The Esquire Tavern is truly a different world from the raucous party happening above. With Hank Cathey coming up with some of the most innovative drinks and drink presentations in the city, Downstairs is an experience in and of its own.

GLASSWARE: Cocktail glass
GARNISH: Strip of orange peel

- **2 oz. Blue Corn Gin (see recipe)**
- **1 oz. Huitlacoche Vermouth (see recipe)**
- **1 oz. Luxardo maraschino liqueur**
- **Dash of Regan's Orange Bitters**
- **Dash of Bittermens Scarborough Bitters**

1. Chill the cocktail glass in the freezer.
2. Place all of the ingredients in a mixing glass, fill it two-thirds of the way with ice, and stir until chilled.
3. Strain the cocktail into the chilled glass.
4. Express the strip of orange peel over the drink, use it as a garnish, and enjoy.

BLUE CORN GIN: Combine 8 oz. landrace blue corn and 1 liter of Greenall's gin. Let the mixture steep for 14 days, agitating it daily. Strain before using or storing.

HUITLACOCHE VERMOUTH: Combine 5 parts Boissiere Extra Dry Vermouth with 1 part Huitlacoche Tincture (see recipe), and use immediately or store at room temperature.

HUITLACOCHE TINCTURE: Combine 2 lbs. huitlacoche and 4 cups Everclear. Let the mixture steep for 24 hours. Strain before using or storing.

THE LITTLEJOHN COBBLER

DAIQUIRI TIME OUT
GALVESTON, TEXAS

This cocktail takes its name from Elbridge Gerry Littlejohn, who was one of the great documentarians of South Texas and the author of *Texas History Stories* and *Geography of Texas*. At DTO, the kumquats used in this cocktail typically come from the property where Littlejohn built his home.

GLASSWARE: Julep mug
GARNISH: Fresh mint, sliced strawberry,
sliced kumquat, confectioners' sugar

- 1½ oz. Kumquat & Strawberry Syrup (see recipe)
- ¾ oz. Pedro Ximénez sherry
- ¾ oz. oloroso sherry
- ¾ oz. Plantation O.F.T.D. Rum
- ¼ oz. fresh lime juice

1. Place all of the ingredients in a cocktail shaker, fill it two-thirds of the way with ice, and shake until chilled.

2. Fill the Julep mug with crushed ice and strain the cocktail over it. Top with more crushed ice.

3. Garnish with fresh mint, the sliced strawberry, sliced kumquat, and confectioners' sugar and enjoy.

KUMQUAT & STRAWBERRY SYRUP: Combine 2 cups sugar and 1 cup water in a saucepan and bring to a simmer, stirring to dissolve the sugar. Add 15 sliced strawberries and 10 sliced kumquats, reduce the heat, and gently simmer until the fruit has collapsed. Remove the pan from heat and let the syrup cool completely. Strain before using or storing in the refrigerator.

JOHNNY'S BOILERMAKER SHOT

This recipe makes about 50 servings, so adjust the amounts based on how big of a crowd you're expecting. Or just go ahead and make what's listed here—it does keep well in the refrigerator.

GLASSWARE: Shot glasses
GARNISH: Orange slices

- 32 oz. Mellow Corn Whiskey
- 10 oz. purified water
- 8 oz. Orange & Cherry Syrup (see recipe)

- 1 oz. Angostura Bitters
- Salt, for the rim
- Sugar, for the rim

1. Place the whiskey, water, syrup, and bitters in a large mason jar and stir to combine. Chill the mixture in the refrigerator for 2 hours.

2. To serve, rim shot glasses with salt and sugar and pour the cocktail into the glasses. Garnish each glass with an orange slice and enjoy.

ORANGE & CHERRY SYRUP: Combine 1 cup cherry syrup from a jar of Luxardo maraschino cherries and 1 orange peel and bring to a gentle simmer. Remove the pan from heat and let the syrup steep until it has cooled completely. Strain before using or storing in the refrigerator.

ROSEWATER SOUR

ROSEWATER
HOUSTON, TEXAS

This is a quick sipper, so watch yourself while consuming.

GLASSWARE: Coupe
GARNISH: Rose tincture

- 2 oz. floral gin (Uncle Val's Restorative or Hendrick's)
- ¾ oz. fresh lemon juice
- ¾ oz. Rosewater Mix (see recipe)
- 1 egg white

1. Place all of the ingredients in a cocktail shaker and dry shake for 15 seconds.

2. Add ice and shake until chilled.

3. Strain into the coupe, garnish with a few drops of rose tincture, and enjoy.

ROSEWATER MIX: Combine 2 parts Red Wine Syrup (see recipe) with 1 part Combier Rose Liqueur and 1 part Orgeat (see page 50).

RED WINE SYRUP: Combine equal parts caster (superfine) sugar and robust red wine and stir until the sugar has dissolved. Add cardamom tincture to taste and use or store in the refrigerator.

THE HATCHBACK

The idea behind Firehouse Lounge was to create a "craft dive" bar. The building itself was Austin's oldest fire station, built in 1885, and Firehouse Lounge is on the first floor of what is now the Firehouse Hostel. That can come in handy if you happen to go a little too hard at the bar.

GLASSWARE: Mason jar
GARNISH: Orange twist, grapefruit slice

- 1½ oz. silver tequila
- ¾ oz. Campari
- ½ oz. fresh lime juice
- ½ oz. fresh ruby red grapefruit juice
- ½ oz. Simple Syrup (see page 20)
- Topo Chico, to top

1. Place all of the ingredients, except for the Topo Chico, in a cocktail shaker, fill it two-thirds of the way with ice, and shake until chilled.
2. Strain the cocktail over ice into the mason jar and top with Topo Chico.
3. Garnish with the orange twist and grapefruit slice and enjoy.

TARRAGUEUR

THE ROOSEVELT ROOM
AUSTIN, TEXAS

Austin's Justin Lavenue is one of the world's best bartenders....Want proof? He won Bombay Sapphire's Most Imaginative Bartender a few years back. That's reason enough to go to The Roosevelt Room, where the massive cocktail menu is broken into various eras and the cocktails invented during each epoch.

GLASSWARE: Nick & Nora glass
GARNISH: 3 Islay Scotch spritzes, fresh tarragon, strip of grapefruit peel

- 1½ oz. Texas whiskey (Balcones Single Malt or Balcones True Blue Cask Strength preferred)
- 1 oz. ruby red grapefruit juice
- ½ oz. Honey Syrup (see page 73)

- Strip of grapefruit peel
- 8 fresh tarragon leaves
- Dash of 10 Percent Saline Solution (see page 313)

1. Place all of the ingredients in a cocktail shaker and muddle.

2. Add 1 large ice cube and shake until chilled.

3. Strain into the Nick & Nora glass, spritz the cocktail with Islay Scotch, garnish with fresh tarragon and the strip of grapefruit peel, and enjoy.

THE NOMAD

ATLAS
DALLAS, TEXAS

A fitting drink to represent Atlas, as its menu takes guests on a tour of global flavors. Despite the worldly concept, Atlas is a neighborhood joint that welcomes one and all.

GLASSWARE: Collins glass
GARNISH: Makrut lime leaf

- 2 oz. Makrut-Infused Townes Vodka (see recipe)
- ½ oz. Simple Syrup (see page 20)
- ½ oz. fresh lime juice
- 1½ oz. unsweetened coconut milk
- 2 dashes of Scrappy's Lavender Bitters
- 1½ oz. JP. Chenet Brut Sparkling Wine

1. Place all of the ingredients, except for the sparkling wine, in a cocktail shaker, fill it two-thirds of the way with ice, and shake until chilled.

2. Strain the cocktail into the Collins glass, add ice, and top with the sparkling wine.

3. Garnish with the makrut lime leaf and enjoy.

MAKRUT-INFUSED TOWNES VODKA: Combine 10 grams makrut lime leaves with 1 liter of Townes Vodka. Let the mixture steep for 24 hours. Strain before using or storing.

TEXAS GENTLEMAN

FIRESTONE & ROBERTSON
FORT WORTH, TEXAS

Warm up with some TX Whiskey and Austin's own Caffe Del Fuego. Think of this as a coffee-centered take on the Old Fashioned.

★

GLASSWARE: Rocks glass
GARNISH: Strip of orange peel

- 2 oz. Firestone & Robertson TX Blended Whiskey
- ½ oz. Caffe del Fuego
- 3 dashes of Fee Brothers Aztec Chocolate Bitters

1. Fill the rocks glass with ice, add all of the ingredients, and stir until chilled.

2. Garnish with the strip of orange peel and enjoy.

THE GREENVILLE GRANNY

ALAMO CLUB
DALLAS, TEXAS

Although it opened in 2019, Alamo Club feels as though it's always been a part of Lowest Greenville. This is a collaboration between Austin Rodgers and one of the OG cocktail bartenders in Dallas, Matt Orth. Alamo Club has a fantastic menu and is very laid-back. For this infusion, make sure you give it a good three to four days before using.

GLASSWARE: Collins glass
GARNISH: Green apple slice, freshly grated nutmeg

- 1½ oz. Green Apple–Infused Vodka (see recipe)
- ¾ oz. Licor 43
- ½ oz. fresh lime juice
- Fever-Tree Ginger Beer, to top

1. Build the cocktail in the Collins glass, adding the vodka, Licor 43, and lime juice. Fill the glass with ice, top with ginger beer, and gently stir.

2. Garnish with the slice of green apple and freshly grated nutmeg and enjoy.

GREEN APPLE–INFUSED VODKA: Combine 3 sliced green apples and 1 liter of Tito's Handmade Vodka and let the mixture steep for 1 week. Strain before using or storing.

BERTA'S CUP

JET-SETTER
SAN ANTONIO, TEXAS

Jet-Setter rose from the ashes of Juniper Tar, one of the best, now gone, cocktail bars in Texas. This incredibly approachable cocktail is Benjamin Krick's cross between a Moscow Mule and a Pimm's Cup, incorporating tropical flavors from Mexico.

GLASSWARE: Clay cup
GARNISH: Cucumber ribbon

- 1½ oz. Uruapan Charanda Blanco Rum
- 1 oz. Jasper's Basic Stock (see recipe)
- ½ oz. fresh cucumber juice
- ½ oz. Passion Fruit Syrup (see page 153)
- Goya Ginger Beer, to top

1. Place all of the ingredients, except for the ginger beer, in a cocktail shaker, fill it two-thirds of the way with ice, and shake until chilled.

2. Strain the cocktail over ice into the clay cup and top with ginger beer.

3. Garnish with the cucumber ribbon and enjoy.

JASPER'S BASIC STOCK: Combine 6 oz. lime juice and ½ cup of piloncillo sugar in a mason jar and stir until the sugar has dissolved. Add ¾ oz. Angostura Bitters and half of a freshly grated nutmeg, seal the mason jar, and shake until the mixture is thoroughly combined. Use immediately or store in the refrigerator for up to 1 month.

OLD TIMER

PEGGY'S ON THE GREEN
BOERNE, TEXAS

Peggy's on the Green is named for the late mother of chef/owner Mark Bohanan, who was a great cook in her own right. Located in the historic Kendall Inn, Peggy's on the Green offers cocktails and elevated comfort food in the Hill Country—basically, it's Texas heaven.

GLASSWARE: Collins glass
GARNISH: Strip of orange peel

- 1½ oz. bourbon
- ½ oz. Cynar
- ½ oz. Punt e Mes vermouth
- ½ oz. fresh lemon juice
- ¼ oz. Simple Syrup (see page 20)
- 4 dashes of Angostura Bitters
- Club soda, to top

1. Place all of the ingredients, except for the club soda, in a cocktail shaker, fill it two-thirds of the way with ice, and shake until chilled.

2. Double-strain the cocktail over ice into the Collins glass and top with club soda.

3. Express the strip of orange peel over the cocktail, use it as a garnish, and enjoy.

EL PAJARO

Space Cowboy is a fun and quirky poolside oasis with tropical drinks and amazing Filipino food. Samantha Ruiz's drink is named after a card in the Mexican bingo game Lotería. The bittersweet and tart Hibiscus Syrup is balanced by the sweetness of the fresh pineapple juice.

GLASSWARE: Collins glass
GARNISH: Brûléed Pineapple (see recipe), fresh mint

- 1 oz. fresh orange juice
- ¼ oz. fresh lime juice
- 1 oz. fresh pineapple juice
- ½ oz. Hibiscus Syrup (see recipe)
- ¼ oz. mezcal
- ¾ oz. Campari
- 1 oz. Plantation 3 Stars Rum

1. Place the orange juice in a blender and pulse to "fluff" the juice. Set the orange juice aside.

2. Build the cocktail in a Collins glass, adding the remaining ingredients in the order they are listed. Fill the glass with crushed ice, leaving a ½ inch of space for the orange juice.

3. Slowly pour the fluffed orange juice over the crushed ice.

4. Garnish the cocktail with the Brûléed Pineapple and fresh mint and enjoy.

BRÛLÉED PINEAPPLE: Simply place some sugar in a dish, roll a pineapple wedge in the sugar until it is coated, and then use a kitchen torch to brûlée the pineapple.

HIBISCUS SYRUP: Place 1 teaspoon loose-leaf hibiscus tea in 1 cup Simple Syrup (see page 20) and steep for 10 days. Strain before using or storing in the refrigerator.

WEST

Pisco Punch ★ Mai Tai ★ Chartreuse Swizzle

Tommy's Margarita ★ Sam Flores ★ Eggnog Punch

In the Pines, Under the Palms ★ Milano ★ Bari Martini

Pamplemousse au Poivre ★ Shinjuku Gardens

Utopia ★ The Beehive ★ Drago Roso ★ Otium

Horchata Painkiller ★ I Plum Forgot

Jacqueline's Revenge ★ The Church ★ Violets Are Blue

Italian Greyhound ★ Marnie ★ Pica Fresa

Perfect Stranger ★ Video Killed the Radio Star

Supernova Lava Burst ★ Mr. Kotter

Home Is Where the Heat Is ★ Carried Away

Piña de Victorioso ★ Ananda Spritz ★ Farm & Vine

Island Hopper ★ Whistlepodu ★ Sea Collins

The Country Lawyer ★ Leeward Negroni ★ Red Temples

Sailor's Guillotine ★ Jardín Fresco ★ Proper Cup

The Expedition ★ Thank You Very Matcha

Asylum Harbor ★ Fortunato's Reviver ★ Guera

Gourmet Lemon ★ Night Vision ★ Circe's Kiss

Time's Arrow II ★ Bali Old Fashioned ★ Negroni Caffe

Tomato Beef ★ Bourbon & Spice ★ The Tough Get Going

Oh, What's That? ★ Rabo de Galo ★ Mr. Coco

Exchange Student ★ Three Wishes ★ Flor de la Piña

Disgruntled Mai Tai

As anyone who has done it knows, the drive across Texas is long and, at times, nerve-wracking, as it is easy for the long expanses of nothing to start messing with your mind—Did that same truck pass me an hour ago? Does my cell have any reception in case I blow out a tire? But knowing that the West, the "Golden Land" lies on the other side is more than enough to push you through the anxiety. In addition to the considerable natural beauty that exists in the West, it is also the land where glitz, glamour, talent, and creativity combine to produce looks and lifestyles that are the envy of the world.

As you might imagine, the cocktail scene in such a place is nothing short of next level. The best of Los Angeles, Las Vegas, and San Francisco are collected here, combining to produce experiences that will linger long in the mind. The City in particular shows out here, in part because its tradition extends slightly further back than most places in the West—Jerry Thomas, the godfather himself, plied his trade there during the Gold Rush—and in part because the contemporary bars and bartenders there seem to be focused more on craft than clicks, an assertion backed up the presence of contemporary industry giants like Nicolas Torres and Martin Cate.

PISCO PUNCH

COMSTOCK SALOON
SAN FRANCISCO, CALIFORNIA

One of San Francisco's most historic locally invented cocktails somehow still isn't an easily found drink around the city. *The* bar in San Francisco to get the definitive Pisco Punch is Comstock Saloon in North Beach (a vintage saloon from The Absinthe Group with classic drinks and the highest quality of ingredients). Comstock is just a few blocks from where the drink was invented by Duncan Nicol at the Bank Exchange, a saloon located along what previously was the Bay's waterfront and where a little landmark called the Transamerica Pyramid stands today. City cocktail history doesn't get more fun than that! If you can find some Small Hand Foods Pineapple Gum Syrup, this is a wonderfully easy recipe for bringing a dash of San Francisco history to your home bar. Just accept the fact that you'll have to improvise the Nicol Juice. As The Absinthe Group's Jonny Raglin says: "I make the secret ingredient and nobody has the recipe except me. It is common knowledge that the key ingredient is makrut lime leaves but there are a number of other things in this tincture. It is called Nicol Juice as a nod to Duncan Nicol, who invented the drink in the nineteenth century here in the city. He took the recipe to his grave."

GLASSWARE: Flip cup
GARNISH: Lemon twist

- 2 oz. pisco
- ¾ oz. Small Hand Foods Pineapple Gum Syrup
- 1 oz. fresh lemon juice
- 3 to 4 dashes of Nicol Juice

1. Place all of the ingredients in a cocktail shaker, fill it two-thirds of the way with ice, and shake until chilled.

2. Double-strain over 1 ice cube into the flip cup, garnish with the lemon twist, and enjoy.

MAI TAI

TRADER VIC'S
OAKLAND, CALIFORNIA

There is some debate over where and when the Mai Tai was created, pitting LA's Don the Beachcomber against SF's Trader Vic's in the cocktail world's version of the Dodgers-Giants rivalry. In the eyes of San Francisco cocktail history, it was Trader Vic Bergeron who invented the Mai Tai while behind the bar of his Oakland restaurant in 1944. He threw together these ingredients to create a new rum drink, added a lime shell for color, and served it to two friends visiting from Tahiti. One of them, Carrie Guild, according to Trader Vic's lore, took a sip and replied, "Mai Tai—Roa Ae." Translated from Tahitian, that means, "Out of this world—the best." And there you have the inspiration for the cocktail name.

Nowadays, it's fairly easy to find the Trader Vic's syrups needed to make this recipe. Rock candy syrup is always the curveball of the equation since it's kind of like simple syrup and kind of not. To complete *the* Trader Vic's Mai Tai, however, it's imperative to have it.

GLASSWARE: Mai Tai glass
GARNISH: Fresh mint, lime shell

- 2 oz. Jamaican rum
- ¾ oz. curaçao
- ½ oz. Trader Vic's Orgeat Syrup
- ¼ oz. fresh lime juice
- ¼ oz. Trader Vic's Rock Candy Syrup
- Juice of ½ lime (reserve spent lime shell for garnish)

1. Place all of the ingredients in a cocktail shaker, fill it two-thirds of the way with ice, and shake until chilled.

2. Pour the contents of the shaker into the Mai Tai glass, garnish with fresh mint and the lime shell, and enjoy.

CHARTREUSE SWIZZLE

CLOCK BAR
SAN FRANCISCO, CALIFORNIA

While the classic cocktails of San Francisco all were created in the middle of the twentieth century or earlier, the most iconic twenty-first century cocktail from the city is the Chartreuse Swizzle. It's very simple, yet so profound. Swizzle (the tropics!) and Green Chartreuse (herbal, tangy, made by Carthusian monks in a secluded part of the French Alps) come together for this drink that is crushable and also an eyebrow-raising curiosity. It's the invention of Marco Dionysos, one of the key figures of the modern cocktail movement, who was "the first *technically* amazing bartender I ever saw," says Bay Area cocktail legend Scott Beattie. "[The Ginger Rogers cocktail] was one of the first not-sweet cocktails I had ever had. It changed my whole perspective on drinks. He was also an incredibly fast bartender. He had created this menu at Absinthe, which had about 40 kinds of resurrected classic cocktails, and the Ginger Rogers was one of them. I was just blown away that there were 40 drinks, none of which I had heard of, and this guy could make them at lightning speed.

A few years later, Dionysos created this drink at the Westin St. Francis's beautiful Clock Bar, and the cocktail can now be found on menus all over the world.

GLASSWARE: Tall swizzle glass
GARNISH: None

- **1½ oz. Green Chartreuse**
- **¾ oz. fresh lime juice**
- **1 oz. pineapple juice**
- **½ oz. Velvet Falernum**

1. Fill the swizzle glass with pebble ice and add all of the ingredients. Use the swizzle method to mix the drink: place a bar spoon between your hands, lower it into the drink, and quickly rub your palms together to rotate the spoon as you move it up and down in the drink. When frost begins to form on the outside of the glass, the drink is mixed.

2. Add more pebble ice if desired and enjoy.

TOMMY'S MARGARITA

TOMMY'S MEXICAN RESTAURANT
SAN FRANCISCO, CALIFORNIA

San Francisco's most renowned cocktail creation isn't even a cocktail that was invented in the city. But it was perfected in San Francisco.

It's a pilgrimage for every cocktail drinker to go to the humble source of what is universally considered the ideal Margarita. While most destinations with such an enormous global following tend to be flashy and happy to let you know how famous they are, Tommy's Mexican Restaurant on busy Geary Boulevard in the oh so diverse Outer Richmond neighborhood is nothing like that. It's a humble place owned by the Bermejo family that has been a city favorite for Mexican cuisine (specifically from the Bermejos' native Yucatán) since Tommy (Tomas) and his wife, Elmy, opened the restaurant in 1965.

A few decades after opening, their son, Julio, shaped Tommy's into a spectacular destination for studying and sipping the four kinds of premium 100% agave tequila—blanco, reposado, añejo, and extra añejo (along with joven, which is a blend of reposado and blanco)—and he also created the Margarita recipe heard round the world. There are three ingredients in this Margarita (and most other versions), and each one matters critically.

And it goes without saying that this Margarita—THE Tommy's Margarita—shall never be blended.

★

GLASSWARE: Rocks glass
GARNISH: None

- Salt, for the rim (optional)
- 2 oz. silver tequila
- ½ oz. agave nectar
- 1 oz. fresh lime juice

1. Wet the rim of the rocks glass and coat it with salt, if desired.

2. Place the remaining ingredients in a cocktail shaker, fill it two-thirds of the way with ice, and shake until chilled.

3. Strain the cocktail over ice into the rocks glass and enjoy.

SAM FLORES

TRICK DOG
SAN FRANCISCO, CALIFORNIA

Don't ever get too attached to a favorite drink at Trick Dog, since the menu rotates every six months. One of those cocktails is this spicy tequila-and-horchata drink from the ninth menu, the Trick Dog Mural Project, when the bar teamed up with fourteen local artists, including Sam Flores himself, to make fourteen murals around the city and name a drink after each artist.

★

GLASSWARE: Small clay pot
GARNISH: Lime wheel, cinnamon stick, fresh mint

- 1½ oz. tequila
- 1 oz. Ancho Reyes
- 2½ oz. Pear & Cardamom Horchata (see recipe)

- ½ oz. fresh lime juice
- Dash of Angostura Bitters

1. Place all of the ingredients in a cocktail shaker, fill it two-thirds of the way with ice, and shake vigorously until chilled.

2. Fill the clay pot with crushed ice and double-strain the cocktail over it.

3. Garnish the cocktail with the lime wheel, cinnamon stick, and fresh mint and enjoy.

PEAR & CARDAMOM HORCHATA: Preheat the oven to 350°F. Place 3½ cinnamon sticks, 14 green cardamom pods, and ¾ of a nutmeg seed on a baking sheet, place it in the oven, and toast the spices for 20 minutes. Remove them from the oven and let them cool. Place 7 cups pear juice, 4 cups water, 4¼ cups jasmine rice, 2 cups honey, 1 vanilla bean, zest of 1 lime, and toasted aromatics in a large container and let the mixture steep at room temperature overnight. Working in batches, place the mixture in a food processor and blitz until smooth. Double-strain the mixture, pressing down on the solids to extract as much liquid as possible. For every 4 cups of horchata, stir in 2 oz. of Cinnamon Syrup (see page 137). Use immediately or store in the refrigerator, where it will keep for up to 1 week.

EGGNOG PUNCH

Guests at the lavish, irresistibly fun Lazy Bear "dinner parties" start with a cocktail reception in the upstairs Den. Many of the city's top chefs and bartenders have passed through the kitchen and bar of David Barzelay's trailblazing pop-up turned restaurant in the Mission. In the spirit of being a communal fine-dining experience, Lazy Bear often serves punch bowl cocktail options (in addition to a host of other intricate creations). What is more festive than eggnog and punch?

GLASSWARE: Tumblers
GARNISH: None

- **4 cups buttermilk**
- **8 cups whole milk**
- **6 cups heavy cream**
- **3 cups aged rum**
- **2¼ cups VSOP brandy**
- **1 tablespoon pumpkin spice**
- **6 eggs, yolks and whites separated**
- **1½ cups sugar**
- **Salt, to taste**

1. In a large container, combine the buttermilk, milk, heavy cream, rum, brandy, and pumpkin spice.

2. Combine the egg yolks and 1 cup of sugar in the work bowl of a stand mixer fitted with the whisk attachment. Whisk the mixture until it is a vibrant yellow. Add the egg yolk mixture to the mixture in the large container and whisk to incorporate.

3. Clean the stand mixer's work bowl and then place the egg whites and remaining sugar in it. Whip until soft peaks form.

4. Gradually fold the egg white mixture into the liquid mixture, which will create a more luscious texture.

5. Chill the eggnog in the refrigerator for 1 hour before serving.

IN THE PINES, UNDER THE PALMS

TRUE LAUREL
SAN FRANCISCO, CALIFORNIA

Rye whiskey and gin, tropics and forests—many different worlds combine in this unique masterpiece by Nicolas Torres at Lazy Bear's relaxed sibling, also in the Mission District. It's a perfect example of Torres's distinct style that emphasizes California nature and clever techniques for achieving new flavor dimensions. "I wanted to make a twist on a local classic while keeping to our ethos of working with local produce," Torres said of this creation. "I decided to do a twist on a Martinez that utilized St. George Terroir Gin. This gin was already inspired by the native plant habitat of Mt. Tamalpais. I had already been foraging redwood shoots for dishes and that seemed like a natural fit to introduce that Northern California essence to the drink. The pairing of coconut and pine came in a dream—I work too much—but it turned out to be a beautiful pairing. We decided to bring that flavor in on a new base and rye whiskey jumped out to us because the Martinez is always a great drink to introduce to whiskey drinkers that claim they don't like gin. It really came together!"

GLASSWARE: Rocks glass
GARNISH: Redwood or pine sprout

- ¾ oz. Oliveros Vermouth
- ¾ oz. St. George Terroir Gin
- ¾ oz. Toasted Coconut Rye (see recipe)
- ¼ oz. Luxardo maraschino liqueur
- ¼ oz. water
- 2 dashes of Angostura Bitters
- 1 redwood or pine sprout

1. Place all of the ingredients in a mixing glass, fill it two-thirds of the way with ice, and stir until chilled.

2. Strain over ice into the rocks glass, garnish with the redwood or pine sprout, and enjoy.

TOASTED COCONUT RYE: Place 4 cups rye whiskey in a large mason jar. Place 2 heaping tablespoons organic coconut oil in a saucepan and warm it over medium heat until it gently simmers. Add 1 cup coconut flakes and remove the pan from heat. Stir the flakes until they start to turn brown. Add the coconut mixture to the mason jar while the oil is still in liquid form. Seal the jar, shake it vigorously, and let the mixture sit for 10 minutes. Shake vigorously, place the jar in the freezer, and let it sit overnight. Remove the fat layer and strain the whiskey before using or storing.

Q & A WITH NICOLAS TORRES

Even with the success David Barzelay and Nicolas Torres had after opening the acclaimed restaurant Lazy Bear in San Francisco's Mission District, they decided Torres's gifts as a mixologist needed room to grow.

Enter True Laurel, a cocktail bar imbued with midcentury whimsy—there is a reason the room's design centerpiece is a wall sculpture inspired by Isamu Noguchi's playscapes—that is reflected in a rotating list of cocktails that celebrates the never-ending abundance of local ingredients.

What can you tell us about how the bar was started?

Chef David and I had been working together for about 3 years at Lazy Bear, and we were always looking for ways to improve the bar program. One day we realized that our ideas may have outgrown what we could do within the confines of Lazy Bear, so we searched for a new space that could focus a little more on drinks, but carry a similar ethos.

What is the theme of the bar and its focus?

I don't think we were going for a theme. Our focus is working with seasons and the farmers that supply our stuff. We want to use the most of the bounty California has to offer, and we want to use what we can get to the extent that we hopefully waste as little as possible. There are definitely bars we looked at for flow and back-of-house operations, but as for look and feel we really took our own path, and found it very important to do so.

What do you look for when creating new cocktails?

I usually start with the produce and work backward. I'm typically looking for ways to use good produce, rare wines, and common spirits. This formula has been good to me. I strive for balance and a certain lightness.

What are the best parts of running a cocktail bar? Are there any downsides or things that make it difficult?

This city is saturated with food and cocktails, it is very gluttonous at times. The hard part is staying competitive. The city is always looking for what's next. It also constantly pushes you as an artist to perform. At the same time, there is so much support in the industry, and we all try to learn from each other.

Blue Hawaiian, Brandy Alexander, Pink Squirrel, Rusty Nail, Tom Collins, White Russian, Grasshopper, Rob Roy, Pink Lady: If you had to pick one of these classic cocktails to add to your cocktail menu, how would you make it fit in with your style?

Tom Collins for sure, I still order them all the time. It's a beautiful cocktail. Like a lot of simple sours, or fizz in this case, the details really matter. Simple yet complex, you can learn so much from that drink. It is the base of so many fizzes, coolers, and daisies that came after it.

Do you have a personal favorite cocktail?

I'm a huge Highball fan, brandy and soda please.

Do you have a favorite spirit to work with when making cocktails?

I think about wines and fortified wines more than I think about spirits, or at least when I'm trying to use a certain spirit I often think what wine would go well with it.

MILANO

LIBERTINE SOCIAL
LAS VEGAS, NEVADA

If you're a fan of orange, especially blood orange, this is the cocktail for you.

GLASSWARE: Champagne flute
GARNISH: None

- 1½ oz. Effen Blood Orange Vodka
- ¾ oz. Aperol
- 1 oz. fresh lemon juice
- ½ oz. Simple Syrup (see page 20)
- ½ oz. egg white
- 1 oz. Prosecco, plus more to top

1. Chill the Champagne flute in the freezer.
2. Place all of the ingredients, except for the Prosecco, in a cocktail shaker containing 1 large ice cube and shake until chilled.
3. Pour the Prosecco into the chilled Champagne flute and strain the cocktail over it.
4. Top with additional Prosecco and enjoy.

BARI MARTINI

BARI
LOS ANGELES, CALIFORNIA

You don't need an olive in your Martini when your gin has been flavored with olive oil.

★

GLASSWARE: Nick & Nora glass
GARNISH: 1 to 2 olive leaves

- 3 oz. Olive Oil–Washed Gin (see recipe)
- 1 lemon peel

1. Place the gin in a mixing glass, fill it two-thirds of the way with ice, and stir until chilled.

2. Strain the gin into the Nick & Nora glass, express the lemon peel over the drink, rub it on the rim of the glass, and discard the lemon peel.

3. Garnish with the olive leaves and enjoy.

OLIVE OIL–WASHED GIN: Place 1 liter of premium gin and ½ cup premium extra-virgin olive oil in a container and chill it in the freezer overnight. Discard the hardened layer, stir in 4 oz. of dry vermouth, and strain the mixture through a coffee filter before using or storing.

PAMPLEMOUSSE AU POIVRE

ELIXIR
SAN FRANCISCO, CALIFORNIA

H. Joseph Ehrmann won the 2018 Cocktail of the Year award with this cocktail at the San Francisco World Spirits Competition. After trying its perfect balance of smoke, spice, and tanginess, you'll understand why.

★

GLASSWARE: Tumbler or cocktail glass
GARNISH: Wide lemon twist sprinkled with crushed pink peppercorns

- 2 oz. mezcal
- 1 oz. Giffard Crème de Pamplemousse
- ½ oz. Elixir de Poivre Cordial (see recipe)
- ½ oz. fresh lemon juice
- Dash of The Bitter Truth Grapefruit Bitters

1. Place all of the ingredients in a cocktail shaker, fill it two-thirds of the way with ice, and shake until chilled.

2. Strain into the tumbler, either over crushed ice and garnished with a sprinkle of pink peppercorns and a wide lemon twist, or up into a cocktail glass and garnished with a grapefruit peel cone filled with pink peppercorns rested on the rim.

ELIXIR DE POIVRE CORDIAL: Place 1 cup Stolen Heart vodka (120 proof), 1 tablespoon pink peppercorns, ¼ teaspoon Sichuan peppercorns, and ½ teaspoon coriander seeds in a mason jar, cover, and let the mixture sit at room temperature for 24 hours. Strain and then mix with Simple Syrup (see page 20) at a 1:1 ratio.

SHINJUKU GARDENS

KATANA
LOS ANGELES, CALIFORNIA

Rarely does a cocktail communicate refreshment and vibrancy at as many levels and as well as this one.

GLASSWARE: Collins glass
GARNISH: Matcha, pumpkin-and-mint bouquet, lime wheel, edible flower

- Sugar, for the rim
- 2 cucumber slices
- 2 oz. Beluga Noble Vodka
- ½ oz. Midori
- ½ oz. Luxardo maraschino liqueur
- ¾ oz. fresh lemon juice
- ½ oz. Simple Syrup (see page 20)
- Fever-Tree Sparkling Lime & Yuzu Tonic Water, to top

1. Wet the rim of the Collins glass and coat it with sugar. Add ice to the rimmed glass.
2. Place all of the remaining ingredients, except the tonic water, in a cocktail shaker and muddle.
3. Add ice and shake until chilled.
4. Strain the cocktail into the rimmed glass and top with tonic water.
5. Garnish with the matcha, bouquet, lime wheel, and edible flower and enjoy.

UTOPIA

SCOTCH 80 PRIME
LAS VEGAS, NEVADA

A perfect combination of pear, walnut, and vanilla bean. This very simple yet warm and velvety blend is a perfect addition to any cocktail party!

★

GLASSWARE: Rocks glass
GARNISH: Dehydrated apple slice

- 1½ oz. Redemption Rye Whiskey
- ½ oz. St. George Spiced Pear Liqueur
- ½ oz. Vanilla Syrup (see page 371)
- 2 dashes of Fee Brothers Black Walnut Bitters

1. Place all of the ingredients in a mixing glass, fill it two-thirds of the way with ice, and stir until chilled.

2. Strain the cocktail over a large ice cube into the rocks glass, garnish with the dehydrated apple slice, and enjoy.

THE BEEHIVE

It isn't easy to follow a legend and win a Super Bowl like Steve Young did after Joe Montana left the 49ers. That was close to the tall task given to The Beehive when it replaced Range, a restaurant that launched the careers of many top San Francisco bartenders and also helped put the Mission on the city's midscale/upscale dining map. Range's former chef/owner Phil West is now part of a formidable team—including star designer/contractor Steve Werney and one of the city's longtime favorite chefs, Arnold Eric Wong, that opened The Beehive (and also owns or co-owns The Treasury and Third Rail).

GLASSWARE: Collins glass
GARNISH: Lemon twist

- 1 oz. soda water
- 1½ oz. The Botanist Islay Dry Gin
- ¾ oz. fresh lemon juice
- ¾ oz. Ginger Solution (see recipe)

- ½ oz. Sarsaparilla-Infused Honey Syrup (see recipe)
- 2 dashes of orange bitters
- 2 dashes of 10 Percent Saline Solution (see recipe)

1. Pour the soda water into the Collins glass.

2. Place the remaining ingredients in a cocktail shaker, fill it two-thirds of the way with ice, and shake until chilled.

3. Strain into the glass and add ice.

4. Garnish with the lemon twist and enjoy.

GINGER SOLUTION: Place ½ cup hot water, ½ cup evaporated cane sugar, and ½ cup freshly pressed ginger juice in a mason jar, stir until the sugar has dissolved, and enjoy.

SARSAPARILLA-INFUSED HONEY SYRUP: Place 2 cups local honey, 1 cup hot water, and 1 oz. Indian sarsaparilla in a mason jar and stir to combine. Let the mixture steep for 24 hours. Strain before using or storing in the refrigerator.

10 PERCENT SALINE SOLUTION: Place 1 oz. of salt in a measuring cup. Add warm water until you reach 10 oz. and the salt has dissolved. Let the solution cool before using or storing.

DRAGO ROSO

BUDDY V'S
LAS VEGAS, NEVADA

PAMA Pomegranate Liqueur and pomegranate molasses are the standouts in this cocktail. Both smell like pomegranate, but the pomegranate molasses has more of the fruity, tart notes pomegranate is famed for. Sweetness from the pineapple juice and spice from the serrano pepper add those extra dimensions that are required to make a cocktail memorable.

GLASSWARE: Collins glass
GARNISH: Slice of candied mango, slice of serrano pepper

- 1 serrano pepper, chopped
- 1¾ oz. Absolut Juice Vodka
- 1 oz. mango juice
- ½ oz. PAMA Pomegranate Liqueur
- ½ oz. pineapple juice
- ¾ oz. pomegranate molasses

1. Place the serrano pepper in a cocktail shaker and muddle.
2. Add ice and the remaining ingredients and shake until chilled.
3. Strain the cocktail over ice into the Collins glass, garnish with the candied mango and slice of serrano pepper, and enjoy.

OTIUM

OTIUM
LOS ANGELES, CALIFORNIA

Leaning into Japanese flavors, this beautifully balanced creation is a smoky-sweet sipper that makes you slow down, think, and appreciate. No wonder it's named after the place.

GLASSWARE: Double rocks glass
GARNISH: Green tea–washed ginger candy

- 1½ oz. Hibiki Harmony Whisky
- ¼ oz. Toki Suntory Whisky
- ¼ oz. L'Orgeat Almond Liqueur
- ¾ oz. fresh lemon juice
- ½ oz. Honey Syrup (see page 73)
- 1 bar spoon yuzu juice extract
- 2 dashes of Miracle Mile Yuzu Bitters

1. Place all of the ingredients in a cocktail shaker, fill it two-thirds of the way with ice, and shake until chilled.

2. Double-strain over a large ice cube into the double rocks glass, garnish with the ginger candy, and enjoy.

HORCHATA PAINKILLER

CANOPY CLUB
LOS ANGELES, CALIFORNIA

Head to the roof of The Shay Hotel in Culver City to sip tropical cocktails poolside at the Canopy Club. It's a great spot any time of day, but sunsets always look better several stories up with a drink in your hand.

GLASSWARE: Collins glass
GARNISH: Pineapple wedge, pineapple leaf

- 1½ oz. reposado tequila
- ½ oz. pineapple rum
- ¼ oz. Licor 43
- 2 oz. pineapple juice
- 1 oz. orange juice
- 1 oz. coconut horchata
- 2 dashes of Angostura Bitters
- Blue curaçao, to top

1. Place all of the ingredients, except for the curaçao, in a cocktail shaker, fill it two-thirds of the way with ice, and shake until chilled.

2. Strain the cocktail over ice into the Collins class and top with curaçao.

3. Garnish with the pineapple wedge and pineapple leaf and enjoy.

I PLUM FORGOT

ADA'S
LAS VEGAS, NEVADA

The wine cooler to end all your worries, thanks to Brachetto, the sweet Italian grape that lends its talents to this drink's topper.

★

GLASSWARE: Rocks glass
GARNISH: Plum Flower (see recipe)

- **2 oz. bourbon**
- **1 oz. Plum Syrup (see recipe)**
- **½ oz. Pasubio Vino Amaro**
- **Brachetto d'Acqui, to top**

1. Place the bourbon, syrup, and amaro in a cocktail shaker, fill it two-thirds of the way with ice, and shake until chilled.

2. Double-strain the cocktail over ice into the rocks glass, top with Brachetto, and garnish with the Plum Flower.

PLUM SYRUP: Place 1 cup plum juice, 1 cup sugar, and 1 tablespoon fresh lemon juice in a saucepan and bring to a simmer, stirring until the sugar has dissolved. Remove the pan from heat and let the syrup cool completely before using or storing.

PLUM FLOWER: Use fresh plum round slices, curled up to resemble a rosette and then placed on a skewer or stick.

JACQUELINE'S REVENGE

AMERICANA
LAS VEGAS, NEVADA

This exceptionally flavorful and ultracrisp drink is ideal for sipping by the pool in the gleaming sunlight.

★

GLASSWARE: Rocks glass
GARNISH: Filthy Black Cherry

- 1½ oz. bourbon
- ½ oz. Simple Syrup (see page 20)
- ¼ oz. Ancho Reyes
- ¼ oz. sweet vermouth
- Dash of chocolate bitters
- 1 oz. apple juice

1. Place all of the ingredients in a cocktail shaker, fill it two-thirds of the way with ice, and shake until chilled.

2. Strain the cocktail over ice into the rocks glass, garnish with the Filthy Black Cherry, and enjoy.

THE CHURCH

LOCANDA
SAN FRANCISCO, CALIFORNIA

L ocanda may now be closed, but this glorious cocktail will go on forever.

★

GLASSWARE: Double rocks glass
GARNISH: Long strip of orange peel

- 1 oz. Aperol
- 1 oz. City of London Gin
- 1 oz. fresh lemon juice
- ½ oz. Small Hand Foods Gum Syrup
- ½ oz. Cocchi Americano

1. Place all of the ingredients in a cocktail shaker, fill it two-thirds of the way with ice, and shake until chilled.
2. Double-strain the cocktail over a large ice cube into the double rocks glass, garnish with the strip of orange peel, and enjoy.

VIOLETS ARE BLUE

NOSTALGIA BAR & LOUNGE
LOS ANGELES, CALIFORNIA

Chris Sayegh, aka The Herbal Chef, opened Nostalgia Bar & Lounge with a clear mission in mind: to evoke the sensibilities of childhood. This is done, in part, with a food and drinks menu that pairs food memories like Capri Sun and Orange Julius with CBD- and terpene-infused cocktails. For some of those recipes, check out The Herbal Chef's cookbook, *Sugar High*. While you wait for that to arrive, try this Bianca Sterling creation, which has a wonderful adult-juice-box quality to it.

GLASSWARE: Large coupe
GARNISH: Dehydrated lemon wheel, edible violet blossom

- 1¾ oz. Nelson's Green Brier Tennessee Whiskey
- ½ oz. Red Wine Reduction (see recipe)
- ½ oz. Chambord Black Raspberry Liqueur
- ½ oz. Giffard Crème de Violette
- ⅓ oz. Giffard Wild Elderflower Liqueur
- ½ oz. blueberry puree
- ¾ oz. fresh lemon juice
- 1 oz. egg white
- 2 drops of 10 Percent Saline Solution (see page 313)
- Strip of lemon peel

1. Place all of the ingredients, except for the strip of lemon peel, in a cocktail shaker and dry shake for 1 minute.

2. Add ice, shake until chilled, and double-strain the cocktail into the coupe.

3. Express the strip of lemon peel over the cocktail and discard the lemon peel.

4. Garnish with the dehydrated lemon wheel and edible violet blossom and enjoy.

RED WINE REDUCTION: Place 1 cup red wine in a saucepan and boil until it has reduced by half. Add ½ cup sugar and stir until it has dissolved. Let the reduction cool completely before using or storing.

ITALIAN GREYHOUND

PRAIRIE
SAN FRANCISCO, CALIFORNIA

Chef and owner Anthony Strong is both one of San Francisco's most eloquent voices for discussing subjects well beyond the restaurant industry, and one of its leading culinary talents. After leading the kitchens at Pizzeria Delfina and Locanda, he ventured out on his own with various pop-up and start-up models before opening his own fire-driven restaurant in the Mission. Prairie's tiny bar focuses on Italian amaro and Japanese whisky, and always features this simple, wonderful aperitivo inspired by Strong's time living in Rome.

GLASSWARE: Rocks glass
GARNISH: Grapefruit wheel

- 1 oz. vodka
- ½ oz. Cappelletti
- ½ oz. St. George Bruto Americano
- Fresh grapefruit juice, to top

1. Place all of the ingredients, except for the grapefruit juice, in the rocks glass, add a giant ice cube, top with grapefruit juice, and stir.

2. Garnish with the grapefruit wheel and enjoy.

MARNIE

LASZLO
SAN FRANCISCO, CALIFORNIA

Laszlo is in its third decade of producing excellent cocktails with fresh juices and homemade syrups—yet they're rarely cited as one of the starting points for the city's modern cocktail movement. That's an unfortunate oversight, but no matter, as their thoughtful serves speak for themselves.

GLASSWARE: Rocks glass or copper mug
GARNISH: Dusting of nutmeg, fresh mint

- **2 oz. Absolut Elyx Vodka**
- **¾ oz. Orgeat (see page 50)**
- **¾ oz. fresh lime juice**
- **¾ oz. Passion Fruit Syrup (see page 153)**
- **Pinch of Maldon sea salt**

1. Place all of the ingredients in a cocktail shaker, fill it two-thirds of the way with ice, and shake until chilled.

2. Fill the glass with crushed ice and strain the cocktail over it.

3. Garnish the cocktail with the nutmeg and fresh mint and enjoy.

PICA FRESA

PETTY CASH
LOS ANGELES, CALIFORNIA

Named in honor of Johnny Cash and Tom Petty (and the cover band that plays their hits), Petty Cash is a taqueria created by Walter Manzke, who credits a youth spent taking trips to Tijuana and enjoying its tacos, tequila, and music as his inspiration.

GLASSWARE: Coupe
GARNISH: Chipotle chile powder

- 1½ oz. tequila
- ½ oz. fresh lemon juice
- ½ oz. Cucumber Syrup (see recipe)
- ½ oz. Pickled Strawberry & Fresno Chile Brine (see recipe)

1. Chill the coupe in the freezer.

2. Place all of the ingredients in a cocktail shaker, fill it two-thirds of the way with ice, and shake until chilled.

3. Strain the cocktail into the chilled coupe, garnish with the chipotle chile powder, and enjoy.

CUCUMBER SYRUP: Place 1 cup freshly pressed cucumber juice and 1 cup caster (superfine) sugar in a blender and puree until the sugar has dissolved. Use immediately or store in the refrigerator.

PICKLED STRAWBERRY & FRESNO CHILE BRINE: Place 1 cup white balsamic vinegar, 1 cup water, 1 teaspoon salt, and ¼ cup sugar in a saucepan and bring to a boil, stirring to dissolve the sugar. Place 10 hulled and quartered strawberries and 2 deseeded, sliced Fresno chiles in a heatproof container. Pour the brine over the strawberries and chiles and let the mixture cool to room temperature. Strain before using or storing in the refrigerator.

PERFECT STRANGER

LOLÓ
SAN FRANCISCO, CALIFORNIA

This unique and funky cocktail from Loló, a chic Mexican restaurant and cocktail bar on Valencia Street, is definitely among the best known in the city for one primary reason: goat's milk. Get past that bit of novelty and it's ultimately a wonderful, clarified milk punch that showcases a little spice punching into Lo-Fi's Dry Vermouth and the sweet-oxidation dual personality of oloroso sherry.

GLASSWARE: Rocks glass
GARNISH: Lemon twist, lime twist

- 1½ oz. Fords Gin
- ¾ oz. Lo-Fi Dry Vermouth
- ¼ oz. Lustau Oloroso Sherry
- ½ oz. fresh lemon juice
- ¼ oz. fresh lime juice

- ½ oz. Simple Syrup (see page 20)
- ¼ oz. pickled jalapeño brine
- 2 dashes of celery bitters
- Pinch of kosher salt
- Goat's milk, as needed

1. Place all of the ingredients, except for the goat's milk, in a mixing glass and stir to combine.

2. Add the goat's milk, about one-fifth of the total amount in the mixing glass. Stir to combine and then strain the mixture through cheesecloth into a jar.

3. Rinse off the cheesecloth and strain the mixture again.

4. Pour over ice into the rocks glass, garnish with the lemon twist and lime twist, and enjoy.

VIDEO KILLED THE RADIO STAR

THE CHANDELIER
LAS VEGAS, NEVADA

The coconut foam is made with coconut milk, black pepper, and cardamom, and it goes wonderfully with the slightly grassy taste of cachaça.

GLASSWARE: Coupe
GARNISH: Edible rice paper with "Pop" or "Bang" printed on it

- 1 oz. Prata Avuá Cachaça
- ½ oz. Giffard Crème de Fruits de la Passion
- ½ oz. Italicus Rosolio di Bergamotto
- 1 oz. fresh lemon juice
- ¾ oz. apricot puree
- ½ oz. Spiced Honey Syrup (see recipe)
- Spiced Coconut Foam, to top (see recipe)

1. Place all of the ingredients, except for the Spiced Coconut Foam, in a cocktail shaker, fill it two-thirds of the way with ice, and shake until chilled.

2. Strain the cocktail into the coupe and top with Spiced Coconut Foam.

3. Garnish with the edible rice paper and enjoy.

SPICED HONEY SYRUP: In a saucepan, combine 1 liter honey, 1 liter water, ¼ cup black peppercorns, 2 cups crushed green cardamom pods, and 6 cinnamon sticks and bring to a boil. Reduce the heat to low and simmer for 20 minutes. Remove the pan from heat and let the syrup cool completely. Strain before using or storing in the refrigerator.

SPICED COCONUT FOAM: Place 1 liter Spiced Honey Syrup, 1 liter Coconut Cream (see recipe), and 1 liter pasteurized egg whites into a charged whipping gun and chill in the refrigerator until ready to use.

COCONUT CREAM: Combine 1 liter half-and-half with 1½ liters Coco Lopez Cream of Coconut and use immediately or store in the refrigerator.

SUPERNOVA LAVA BURST

BROKEN SHAKER
LOS ANGELES, CALIFORNIA

Broken Shaker came to LA to make its mark and quickly made itself at home. One of the nation's four acclaimed Freehand hotel bars, Broken Shaker's rooftop poolside setting offers sweeping views of the city and a fun, laid-back ambience. But don't let the vibe fool you: this is a serious cocktail bar with a notable cocktail program that is a favorite of the L.A. Spirits Awards team. The bar's charismatic beverage director, Christine Wiseman, began as a chef but after craving a change, found herself behind the bar. You can still see her culinary background in her cocktail recipes, each with layers of flavor and components that make those flavors shine.

GLASSWARE: Collins glass
**GARNISH: Slice of pineapple crescent, edible flower,
edible glitter (optional)**

- 1 oz. Bombay Sapphire Gin
- ½ oz. Chinola Passion Fruit Liqueur
- ½ oz. Ancho Reyes Verde
- 1 oz. Pineapple & Cacao Nib Shrub (see recipe)
- ¾ oz. fresh lemon juice

1. Place all of the ingredients in a cocktail shaker, fill it two-thirds of the way with ice, and shake until chilled.

2. Strain the cocktail over ice into the Collins glass, garnish with the pineapple crescent, edible flower, and, if desired, edible glitter, and enjoy.

PINEAPPLE & CACAO NIB SHRUB: Combine 2 chopped pineapples (with the skin still on), 4 quarts sugar, 4 quarts rice wine vinegar, 4 quarts water, and 100 grams cacao nibs in a pot, bring to a simmer, and cook for 15 minutes, stirring occasionally. Transfer the mixture to a container and let it steep overnight. Strain before using or storing in the refrigerator.

MR. KOTTER

SCHOOL NIGHT
SAN FRANCISCO, CALIFORNIA

Enrique Sanchez is undoubtedly one of San Francisco's present-day bar legends. After coming to study in San Francisco from his native Peru, Sanchez shifted to the cocktail industry, starting a career of nearly two decades as a bartender or bar manager for several important local restaurant cocktail programs, like La Mar, Beretta, and Arguello. Now he's running the show at Traci Des Jardins's weeknight-only bar, School Night. That's right, it's open only on school nights, and it's well worth putting on the calendar for a rare weeknight out.

GLASSWARE: Rocks glass
GARNISH: Orange slice

- **2 oz. Tapatio Tequila**
- **½ oz. Pierre Ferrand Dry Curaçao**
- **1 oz. fresh lime juice**
- **¼ oz. agave nectar**

1. Place all of the ingredients in a cocktail shaker, fill it two-thirds of the way with ice, and shake vigorously until chilled.

2. Double-strain over a Hibiscus Ice Cube (see recipe) into the rocks glass, garnish with the orange wedge, and enjoy.

HIBISCUS ICE CUBES: Place 8 cups water, 1 cup hibiscus blossoms, and an entire orange peel in a saucepan and bring to a boil. Remove the pan from heat and let the mixture steep for 3 hours. Strain, pour the strained liquid into ice molds, and freeze.

TAMARIND SYRUP: Place ¼ cup tamarind pulp, 1 cup water, and 1 cup sugar in a saucepan and bring to a simmer, stirring to dissolve the sugar and incorporate the tamarind. Remove the pan from heat and let the mixture cool completely. Strain before using or storing.

HOME IS WHERE THE HEAT IS

BESHARAM
SAN FRANCISCO, CALIFORNIA

Heena Patel is an absolute force of creativity and joyful exuberance, always smiling when cooking her unique style of Gujarati food or chatting with guests at her Dogpatch restaurant, Besharam. The cocktails at the restaurant wonderfully reflect the spirit of the food program, like in this mezcal-tamarind cocktail full of heat.

★

GLASSWARE: Double rocks glass
GARNISH: Dehydrated jalapeño slice

- **Lava salt, for the rim**
- **Cumin, for the rim**
- **1½ oz. Spicy Mezcal (see recipe)**
- **¼ oz. Giffard Banane du Brésil**
- **½ oz. fresh lime juice**
- **½ oz. manzanilla sherry**
- **¾ oz. Tamarind Syrup (see recipe)**

1. Place lava salt and cumin in a dish and stir to combine. Wet the rim of the double rocks glass and coat it with the mixture.

2. Place the remaining ingredients in a cocktail shaker, fill it two-thirds of the way with ice, and shake until chilled.

3. Strain over ice into the rimmed glass, garnish with the dehydrated slice of jalapeño, and enjoy.

SPICY MEZCAL: Place sliced jalapeño in a bottle of mezcal and let it steep for 24 hours—determine the amount of jalapeños and the length of time you steep the mixture based on your spice tolerance. Strain before using or storing, and reserve the leftover jalapeños to garnish other cocktails or serve as a boozy and yummy snack.

CARRIED AWAY

Alicia Walton brings together two totally different worlds (aquavit and coconut) in one crisply constructed cocktail. It's easy to get carried away by this one, and order a second round immediately.

GLASSWARE: Snifter

GARNISH: Lime wheels, freshly grated cinnamon

- 1½ oz. Krogstad Aquavit
- ½ oz. fresh lemon juice
- ¾ oz. Clément Mahina Coconut Liqueur
- ¼ oz. Honey Syrup (see page 73)

1. Place all of the ingredients in a cocktail shaker, fill it two-thirds of the way with ice, and shake until chilled.

2. Strain over ice into the snifter, garnish with lime wheels and cinnamon, and enjoy.

PIÑA DE VICTORIOSO

SOL AGAVE
LOS ANGELES, CALIFORNIA

Sol Agave started out as a taco truck before its metamorphosis into a brick-and-mortar restaurant. Its founders, Jesus Galvez and Chef Manny Velasco, now have several award-winning restaurants, including one in the mammoth L.A. Live entertainment complex, and Sol Agave has equally evolved into a serious source of upscale cocktails.

★

GLASSWARE: Cocktail glass
GARNISH: Pineapple leaves

- **Tajín, for the rim**
- **3 slices of roasted pineapple**
- **2 oz. Victorioso Espadín Mezcal**
- **1 oz. fresh lime juice**
- **1 oz. pineapple juice**
- **1 slice of jalapeño pepper**

1. Wet the rim of the cocktail glass and coat it with Tajín. Add ice to the rimmed glass.

2. Place the pineapple in a cocktail shaker and muddle.

3. Add ice and the remaining ingredients and shake until chilled.

4. Strain the cocktail into the rimmed glass, garnish with pineapple leaves, and enjoy.

ANANDA SPRITZ

BURMA CLUB
SAN FRANCISCO, CALIFORNIA

The Outer Richmond's Burma Superstar has been a San Francisco dining staple since the early 1990s. As Bay Area crowds are just as hungry for the tea leaf salad as they've ever been, the original restaurant has slowly morphed into a group with a few different concepts. Their three-story SoMa restaurant, Burma Club, is certainly the glitziest of that roster and features notable cocktails, like this intriguing spritz of pineapple, bourbon, amaro, and bubbles.

GLASSWARE: Cocktail glass
GARNISH: Edible flower blossoms

- 5 pineapple chunks
- 1½ oz. Knob Creek Bourbon
- 1 oz. Amaro Nonino
- 3 dashes of Angostura Bitters
- ½ oz. Demerara Syrup (see page 63)
- ½ oz. fresh lemon juice
- ½ oz. pineapple juice
- ¾ oz. sparkling wine

1. Place the pineapple in a cocktail shaker and muddle it.
2. Add all of the remaining ingredients, except for the sparkling wine, fill the shaker two-thirds of the way with ice, and shake until chilled.
3. Strain the cocktail into the cocktail glass and top with the sparkling wine.
4. Garnish with edible flower blossoms and enjoy.

SUGAR SNAP PEA SYRUP: Place ½ cup water in a saucepan and bring it to a boil. Add 1 lb. sugar and stir until it has dissolved. Remove the pan from heat and let the syrup cool. Stir in 5⅓ oz. sugar snap pea juice and use immediately or store in the refrigerator.

FARM & VINE

NIKU STEAKHOUSE
SAN FRANCISCO, CALIFORNIA

Outside of Martinis at Harris' and the House of Prime Rib, San Francisco isn't really a steakhouse-and-cocktails kind of town. Remember, after all, that nothing pairs better with some red meat than a bold Napa Cabernet Sauvignon. The city's newest and splashiest steakhouse, Niku Steakhouse, focuses on Wagyu cuts, which obviously go well with red wine or Martinis, but also pair nicely with some of the city's most innovative cocktails. According to bar manager Ilya Romanov, "This unique cocktail features a pantry full of ingredients that you typically find dusting up at a bar and rarely find a use for."

GLASSWARE: Rocks glass
GARNISH: Shiso leaf, Umeboshi Powder (see recipe)

- 1 oz. aquavit
- ¾ oz. manzanilla sherry
- ½ oz. verjus
- ¾ oz. fresh lime juice
- ¾ oz. Sugar Snap Pea Syrup (see recipe)
- ½ oz. egg white
- 1 oz. Q Elderflower Tonic

1. Place all of the ingredients, except for the elderflower tonic, in a cocktail shaker and dry shake for 10 seconds.

2. Fill the cocktail shaker two-thirds of the way with ice and shake until chilled.

3. Add the elderflower tonic to the cocktail shaker, strain the cocktail into the rocks glass, and add a few ice cubes.

4. Garnish the cocktail with the shiso leaf and Umeboshi Powder and enjoy.

UMEBOSHI POWDER: Using a dehydrator on a setting for vegetables, spread pitted and pickled umeboshi plums on a tray and dehydrate for 3 days. This will produce a perfectly dry plum, which can then be ground into a powder.

ISLAND HOPPER

TRAILBLAZER TAVERN
SAN FRANCISCO, CALIFORNIA

Freshly pressed Hawaiian sugarcane produces some fantastic rum, and fortunately, there is a small crop of exciting distilleries that are taking advantage of the local produce, like Oahu's Kō Hana Distillers.

GLASSWARE: Collins glass
GARNISH: Pineapple leaves, dehydrated lime wheel

- 1 oz. Don Q Cristal Rum
- ½ oz. Kō Hana Kea Agricole Rum
- ½ oz. fresh lemon juice
- ½ oz. Hibiscus Syrup (see page 282)
- ¾ oz. pineapple juice
- 2 oz. ginger beer

1. Place all of the ingredients, except the ginger beer, in a cocktail shaker, fill it two-thirds of the way with ice, and shake until chilled.

2. Place the ginger beer in the Collins glass, strain the cocktail into the glass, and fill it with crushed ice.

3. Garnish the cocktail with the pineapple leaves and dehydrated lime wheel and enjoy.

MASALA WATER: Place 2 oz. dried mango in a bowl of hot water and soak it for 30 minutes. Place the rehydrated mango, 3 oz. cilantro, 3 green chile peppers, ½ teaspoon black pepper, ¼ teaspoon grated fresh ginger, and 2 teaspoons dried mint in a food processor and blitz until the mixture is a smooth paste. Stir the paste into 4 cups water and use as desired.

WHISTLEPODU

ROOH
SAN FRANCISCO & PALO ALTO, CALIFORNIA

With locations in SoMa and Palo Alto, ROOH is one of the Bay Area's defining contemporary Indian restaurants. There are all sorts of modern techniques involved in the cocktails and food (like carbonation for this cocktail), but it's always to enhance the core purpose of each dish and drink. It isn't glitzy just to be glitzy. Here's head mixologist Chetan Gangan to describe this not-so-typical Bloody Mary: "Whistlepodu means 'to cheer' by blowing a whistle. It's our take on a Bloody Mary, with traditional rasam, which is a spicy and sour tomato soup from southern India."

★

GLASSWARE: Rocks glass
GARNISH: Fried curry leaf

- 2 oz. Smoked Rasam (see recipe)
- 2 oz. vodka
- ¾ oz. honey
- ¾ oz. fresh lime juice
- 1 oz. club soda

1. Place all of the ingredients in a mixing glass, stir to combine, and then carbonate the cocktail.

2. Pour the cocktail over ice into the rocks glass, garnish with the fried curry leaf, and enjoy.

SMOKED RASAM: Dice 15 tomatoes, place them in a saucepan, and cook over medium heat for about 20 minutes. Add coriander seeds, curry leaves, mustard seeds, and Masala Water (see recipe), stir to combine, and remove the pan from heat. Place the saucepan in a large roasting pan. Place hickory wood chips in a ramekin, coat a strip of paper towel with canola oil, and insert it in the center of the wood chips. Set the ramekin in the roasting pan, carefully light the wick, and wait until the wood chips ignite. Cover the roasting pan with aluminum foil and smoke the rasam for 1 hour.

SEA COLLINS

HOG ISLAND OYSTER CO.
SAN FRANCISCO, CALIFORNIA

The good folks at Oakland Spirits Company certainly have fun with their gin. Their Halfshell Gin is a London Dry style, for which 200 Hog Island Sweetwater oysters are crushed in the distilling process. For this version of a coastally inspired Tom Collins, the Oakland Spirits Company Automatic Sea Gin is the drink's briny anchor, packed with foraged nori, lemongrass, and some other elements of California's coastal terroir.

GLASSWARE: Collins glass
GARNISH: 2 or 3 nori sheets, shredded

- 2 oz. Oakland Spirits Company Automatic Sea Gin
- ¾ oz. Seaweed-Infused Honey (see recipe)
- ½ oz. fresh lemon juice
- ½ oz. fresh lime juice
- 4 dashes of chamomile tincture
- Soda water, to top

1. Place all of the ingredients, except for the soda water, in a cocktail shaker, fill it two-thirds of the way with ice, and shake until chilled.

2. Double-strain into the Collins glass, top with soda water, and gently stir.

3. Garnish with the shredded nori and enjoy.

SEAWEED-INFUSED HONEY: Place ½ cup honey and ½ cup water in a mason jar and stir until well combined. Add dried nori and let the mixture sit at room temperature. Strain before using or storing, making sure to press down on the nori to extract as much liquid and flavor as possible.

THE COUNTRY LAWYER

PARK TAVERN
SAN FRANCISCO, CALIFORNIA

There is no finer digestif cocktail in San Francisco than this Big Night Restaurant Group's classic bourbon-amaro-vermouth sipper, created by Casey Doolin way back in 2011.

★

GLASSWARE: Cocktail glass
GARNISH: Strip of orange peel

- 1½ oz. Four Roses Bourbon
- ¼ oz. Bénédictine
- ½ oz. Zucca Rabarbaro Amaro
- Dash of chocolate bitters
- ½ oz. Dolin Blanc

1. Place all of the ingredients in a mixing glass, fill it two-thirds of the way with ice, and stir until chilled.

2. Strain the cocktail into the cocktail glass, garnish with the strip of orange peel, and enjoy.

LEEWARD NEGRONI

PACIFIC COCKTAIL HAVEN
SAN FRANCISCO, CALIFORNIA

San Francisco's most celebrated Negroni isn't exactly your normal gin-sweet vermouth-Campari creation. It isn't even a straight 1:1:1 ratio of the trio. Kevin Diedrich created this masterpiece for Negroni Week one year, and it hasn't left the menu at PCH since.

GLASSWARE: Rocks glass
GARNISH: Pandan leaf

- Bittermens 'Elemakule Tiki Bitters, to rinse
- 1 oz. Coconut Oil–Washed Campari (see recipe)
- ¾ oz. Pandan Cordial (see recipe)
- ½ oz. Sipsmith V.J.O.P. Gin

1. Rinse a rocks glass with bitters, and then discard the bitters.

2. Place the remaining ingredients in a mixing glass, fill it two-thirds of the way with ice, and stir until chilled.

3. Strain over a large ice cube into the rocks glass, garnish with the pandan leaf, and enjoy.

COCONUT OIL–WASHED CAMPARI: Place 2 cups virgin coconut oil and 4 cups Campari in a large mason jar and let it sit at room temperature for 24 hours, stirring occasionally. Place the mixture in the freezer overnight. Remove the solidified layer of fat and strain the Campari through a coffee filter before using or storing.

PANDAN CORDIAL: Place 10 sliced pandan leaves and 4 cups Everclear in a large mason jar and steep for 48 hours. Strain and add 1½ cups Simple Syrup (see page 20) for every 1 cup of tincture.

RED TEMPLES

CREATED BY CHRISTIAN SUZUKI
SAN FRANCISCO, CALIFORNIA

For this cocktail, Christian Suzuki uses shochu as the base, then takes the drinker for a wild, yet elegant, ride full of fruit, bitterness, nuttiness, floral notes, and smoke. It's got it all in beautiful harmony. That seems fitting with the inspiration coming from the magnificent Sensoji Temple in the Asakusa district of Tokyo, which is Suzuki's hometown.

GLASSWARE: Rocks glass
GARNISH: Torched cinnamon stick, maraschino cherries

- 1 strawberry
- 1 oz. Iichiko Saiten Shochu
- ¾ oz. Campari
- ¾ oz. amontillado sherry
- ¼ oz. St-Germain
- 5 dashes of peaty Scotch

1. Place the strawberry in a mixing glass and muddle.

2. Add the remaining ingredients and ice and stir until chilled.

3. Double-strain over ice into the rocks glass, garnish with the torched cinnamon stick and maraschino cherries, and enjoy.

Q & A WITH CHRISTIAN SUZUKI

Where doesn't Christian Suzuki work? If you've been to any of the top bars in San Francisco, I guarantee that you've encountered this star bartender somewhere.

As the COVID-19 pandemic struck, he was working shifts at Wildhawk, Elda, The Treasury, and Benjamin Cooper. And he has his own pop-up, Kagano. I'm sure you'll be seeing a permanent bar from this ultratalented bartender soon.

How did you get your start in bartending and designing drinks? Any particular mentors or influences that are still impactful on what you do today?

I've always been in restaurant hospitality. I kind of grew up into it. My grandparents had a very well-known restaurant business in Tokyo. Their first restaurant, Aramasa, opened right after World War II ended. Its focus was northern Japanese cuisine. My grandfather got a lot of recognition for traveling back to northern Japan to collect local ingredients and also using fresh produce and seafood. My grandparents together opened two more Aramasa locations, a teppanyaki steak house called Sukizuki, a ranch that sourced all of the company's produce and proteins, and of course, Kagano Bar—the cocktail bar my grandmother ran during the '50s and '60s. My grandparents would have me return to Japan up to three times a year from ages 11 to 18 to study Japanese hospitality, food, and management, and then I moved there for over a year. During that time, I was trying to attend an art school in Tokyo but failed to get in. When I returned to the States, I wanted to get my foot into bar hospitality, so I applied for a job at 15 Romolo when I was 21. There I went under the wings of Jared Anderson, Aaron Gregory Smith, and Ian Adams. They taught me to be the most excellent cocktail server, then manager.

When you think of San Francisco cocktail history, what comes to mind?

Many, many decades of many, many hangovers.

Any standout lessons or experiences from the many acclaimed bars you've worked at, like Benjamin Cooper, Elda, and 15 Romolo?

Not to be a square and be friendly. Those two mentalities behind the bar have helped me create so many incredible bonds with guests, coworkers, brand folks, and employers.

SAILOR'S GUILLOTINE

TONGA ROOM & HURRICANE BAR
SAN FRANCISCO, CALIFORNIA

Chartreuse and absinthe in a tiki cocktail? Yes, it's a wonderfully orchestrated, albeit unexpected, cocktail. Enjoy, and I'm guessing you'll be singing with the band and me in the Tonga Room after the next "rainstorm."

GLASSWARE: Tiki mug
GARNISH: Fresh mint, star anise pod

- ¼ oz. Emperor Norton Absinthe
- 1 oz. La Favorite Rhum Agricole
- ½ oz. Velvet Falernum
- ½ oz. Green Chartreuse
- 1 oz. fresh pineapple juice
- ¾ oz. fresh lime juice

1. Place all of the ingredients in a cocktail shaker, fill it two-thirds of the way with ice, and shake until chilled.

2. Pour the contents of the shaker into the tiki mug and top with crushed ice.

3. Garnish with fresh mint and the star anise pod and enjoy.

JARDÍN FRESCO

BORRACHA
LAS VEGAS, NEVADA

Even if you elect to eschew the jalapeño, there is no denying the wonderfully vegetal quality of this cocktail, which is brought to life by the Prosecco float.

★

GLASSWARE: Margarita coupe
GARNISH: Cucumber slice, fresh cilantro, jalapeño slices

- 5 cucumber slices
- 1 jalapeño pepper slice (optional)
- 1 sprig of fresh cilantro

- 1½ oz. Casamigos Blanco Tequila
- ¾ oz. St-Germain
- 1 oz. fresh lime juice
- 2 oz. Prosecco, to float

1. Place the cucumber, jalapeño (if desired), and cilantro in a cocktail shaker and muddle.

2. Add ice and the tequila, St-Germain, and lime juice, shake until chilled, and double-strain the cocktail into the Margarita coupe.

3. Float the Prosecco on top of the cocktail, pouring over the back of a spoon. Garnish with the slice of cucumber, fresh cilantro, and jalapeño and enjoy.

PROPER CUP

CHARMAINE'S
SAN FRANCISCO, CALIFORNIA

When enjoying the view from the San Francisco Proper Hotel's glamorous rooftop hot spot, why not enjoy a clever riff on a Pimm's Cup?

★

GLASSWARE: Footed pilsner glass
GARNISH: Lemon wheel, lime wheel, apple slices, fresh mint

- **2 cucumber ribbons**
- **2 oz. Pimm's**
- **¾ oz. Hendrick's Gin**
- **Dash of Angostura Bitters**
- **2 dashes of Peychaud's Bitters**
- **½ oz. fresh lemon juice**
- **½ oz. fresh lime juice**
- **1 oz. Apple Syrup (see recipe)**
- **Ginger beer, to top**

1. Place the cucumber ribbons in the footed pilsner glass.

2. Place all of the remaining ingredients, except for the ginger beer, in a cocktail shaker, fill it two-thirds of the way with ice, and shake vigorously 20 times.

3. Strain into the glass and top with ginger beer.

4. Garnish with the lemon wheel, lime wheel, apple slices, and fresh mint and enjoy.

APPLE SYRUP: Slice an apple and place it in a medium saucepan with 1 cup water, 1 cup sugar, and ½ teaspoon pure vanilla extract. Bring to a boil over medium heat, reduce the heat to medium-low, and simmer for 5 minutes. Remove the pan from heat and let the syrup cool completely. Strain before using or storing.

THE EXPEDITION

SMUGGLER'S COVE
SAN FRANCISCO, CALIFORNIA

Your home bar might not have the waterfalls and spectacular rum collection of Martin Cate's world-renowned rum paradise on Gough Street in Hayes Valley. Luckily, with a few syrups, a black blended rum, and a big ol' tiki mug, you can certainly produce this delightful Cate creation. In his words: "This drink is called The Expedition, and it's a celebration of the ingredients that Donn Beach, the godfather of tiki, was exposed to and celebrated—coffee and bourbon from New Orleans, fresh citrus from California, and rum and spices from the Caribbean."

GLASSWARE: Tiki mug

GARNISH: Edible orchid blossom

- 2 oz. black blended rum (such as Coruba, Goslings, or Hamilton 86)
- 1 oz. bourbon
- ¼ oz. Bittermens New Orleans Coffee Liqueur
- 1 oz. fresh lime juice
- ½ oz. Cinnamon Syrup (see page 137)
- ½ oz. Honey Syrup (see page 73)
- ¼ oz. Vanilla Syrup (see recipe)
- 2 oz. seltzer

1. Place all of the ingredients in a cocktail shaker, add crushed ice and 4 to 6 small "agitator" cubes, and flash mix with a hand blender.

2. Pour the contents of the shaker into the tiki mug.

3. Garnish with the edible orchid blossom and enjoy.

VANILLA SYRUP: Place 1 cup water in a small saucepan and bring to a boil. Add 2 cups sugar and stir until it has dissolved. Remove the pan from heat. Halve 1 vanilla bean and scrape the seeds into the syrup. Cut the vanilla bean pod into thirds and add the pieces to the syrup. Stir to combine, cover the pan, and let the mixture sit at room temperature for 12 hours. Strain the syrup through cheesecloth before using or storing.

THANK YOU VERY MATCHA

HEARTHSTONE
LAS VEGAS, NEVADA

If you plan on ordering this at Hearthstone, do yourself a favor and grab a spot out on the patio. And be sure to sample the food.

GLASSWARE: Stemless copper wineglass
GARNISH: Lemon wheel, fresh mint

- 1½ oz. Bulldog Gin
- 1 oz. Matcha Agave (see recipe)
- ½ oz. fresh lemon juice
- 3 sprigs of fresh mint
- 2 oz. Champagne, to top

1. Place all of the ingredients, except for the Champagne, in a cocktail shaker, fill it two-thirds of the way with ice, and shake until chilled.

2. Strain the cocktail over ice into the wineglass and top with the Champagne.

3. Garnish with the lemon wheel and fresh mint and enjoy.

MATCHA AGAVE: Place 2 cups water in a saucepan and bring to a boil. Remove from heat, stir in 4 cups dark agave nectar and ¼ cup ground matcha, and let the mixture steep for 15 minutes. Strain the mixture and let it cool completely before using or storing in the refrigerator.

ASYLUM HARBOR

WHITECHAPEL
SAN FRANCISCO, CALIFORNIA

For Martin Cate's second bar in San Francisco, which he opened with bartender Alex Smith and restaurateur John Park, gin is the focus, amidst the backdrop of a grand, almost ominously neglected Victorian-era London Underground station—decidedly more aesthetically pleasing than the actual underground stations in San Francisco.

GLASSWARE: Collins glass
GARNISH: Peychaud's Bitters, freshly grated nutmeg, fresh mint, grapefruit twist

- 1¼ oz. Damrak Gin
- ½ oz. Bénédictine
- ¼ oz. almond liqueur
- 1 bar spoon of St. Elizabeth Allspice Dram
- ½ oz. Ginger Syrup (see page 129)
- ½ oz. passion fruit puree
- ½ oz. fresh lime juice
- ¾ oz. grapefruit juice

1. Place all of the ingredients in a cocktail shaker, fill it two-thirds of the way with ice, and shake until chilled.

2. Strain over ice into the Collins glass, garnish with the bitters, nutmeg, fresh mint, and grapefruit twist, and enjoy.

FORTUNATO'S REVIVER

THE ICE CREAM BAR
SAN FRANCISCO, CALIFORNIA

Who doesn't love a great soda fountain treat? Juliet Pries's excellent all things-ice cream destination in Cole Valley is beloved by all ages for myriad reasons, from malts and milkshakes to the 1930s soda fountain that was driven to San Francisco from its original home in Mackinaw City, Michigan. Plus, it serves "remedies"—low-proof ice cream cocktail delights for the adults. Are they a dessert and a cocktail? Or do they just count as one or the other, and it's okay to then also get a sundae or a beer?

GLASSWARE: Large tulip glass
GARNISH: Toasted black walnuts

- 1½ oz. Bodegas Yuste Aurora Amontillado Sherry
- ½ oz. Cocchi Vermouth di Torino
- ½ oz. Demerara Syrup (see page 63)

- 3½ oz. vanilla ice cream
- 3½ oz. honey ice cream
- 3 tablespoons chopped black walnuts, lightly toasted

1. Chill the tulip glass in the freezer.

2. Place all of the ingredients in a blender and puree until smooth.

3. Pour the drink into the chilled glass, garnish with toasted black walnuts, and enjoy.

GUERA

In the heart of apple and wine country, The Barlow in Sebastopol is a food-and-drink paradise of various restaurants, artisans, breweries, and more. Fern Bar is the resident cocktail bar, and it's a stunner both visually in the plant-filled space and with what you'll be served. This is its excellent take on a Paloma.

GLASSWARE: Collins glass
GARNISH: Grapefruit wheel, lime wheel, dehydrated grapefruit chip

- 1½ oz. tequila
- 1 oz. grapefruit juice
- ¾ oz. fresh lime juice
- ¼ oz. Aperol
- ¼ oz. St-Germain
- ¼ oz. Thai Pepper Shrub (see recipe)
- Fever-Tree Bitter Lemon Soda, to top

1. Place all of the ingredients, except for the soda, in the Collins glass, add ice, and stir until chilled.

2. Top with soda, garnish with the grapefruit wheel, lime wheel, and dehydrated grapefruit chip, and enjoy.

THAI PEPPER SHRUB: Place 4 chopped Thai chile peppers, ¼ cup cane vinegar, and ¼ cup cane sugar in a saucepan and bring to a boil. Cook for 5 minutes, remove the pan from heat, and let the shrub cool completely. Strain before using or storing.

GOURMET LEMON

PARTAGE
LAS VEGAS, NEVADA

This drink doubles as a dessert, thanks to the torched meringue floating on top.

★

GLASSWARE: Coupe

GARNISH: Fresh mint, dehydrated lemon wheel

- 1½ oz. silver tequila
- ¾ oz. limoncello
- ¾ oz. fresh lime juice
- 2 dashes of lemon bitters
- Meringue (see recipe), to top

1. Place all of the ingredients, except for the Meringue, in a mixing glass, fill it two-thirds of the way with ice, and stir until chilled.

2. Strain the cocktail into the coupe, top with the Meringue, and brown the Meringue with a kitchen torch.

3. Garnish with fresh mint and the dehydrated lemon wheel and enjoy.

MERINGUE: Whip 4 large, room-temperature egg whites until they are glossy and begin to hold soft peaks. Add ¼ teaspoon cream of tartar and then slowly beat in ¼ cup of sugar. Beat until the mixture is smooth and can hold stiff peaks.

NIGHT VISION

Healdsburg is quite possibly California's quintessential wine country town. There are stellar wineries and tasting rooms, then acres and acres of vineyards in every direction—plus a cute central plaza in the "downtown," complete with a gazebo. One of the storefronts on the plaza happens to be Duke's, a treasure that is beloved by discerning cocktail drinkers, tourists who are tired of Zinfandel, and many wine and tourism industry workers who are looking to relax with a cold beer or a unique carrot-and-gin cocktail creation.

GLASSWARE: Cocktail glass
GARNISH: Fresh carrot frond

- 1½ oz. Spirit Works Barrel Gin
- 1 oz. Fresh Carrot Juice Syrup (see recipe)
- ½ oz. fresh lemon juice

- ¼ oz. Bordiga Extra Dry Vermouth
- 2 dashes of oloroso sherry
- 2 dashes of Caraway Tincture (see recipe)

1. Chill the cocktail glass in the freezer.

2. Place all of the ingredients in a cocktail shaker, fill it two-thirds of the way with ice, and shake for 15 seconds.

3. Double-strain the cocktail into the chilled cocktail glass, garnish with the carrot frond, and enjoy.

FRESH CARROT JUICE SYRUP: Place 1 cup freshly pressed carrot juice and ½ cup Simple Syrup (see page 20) in a mason jar, stir to combine, and use as desired.

CARAWAY TINCTURE: Place 2 tablespoons caraway seeds and 4 oz. high-proof neutral grain alcohol in a mason jar and steep for at least 24 hours, shaking periodically. Strain before using or storing.

CIRCE'S KISS

Seats are tough to come by at the Downtown Cocktail Room, but they are well worth waiting for, as one puts you well within reach of well-made drinks like the Circe's Kiss. Floral, herbaceous, and slightly sweet, this mystical and botanical potion is sure to put you under its enchanting spell.

GLASSWARE: Coupe

GARNISH: Chamomile blossoms, ground freeze-dried raspberries

- 1½ oz. gin
- ¼ oz. absinthe
- ¾ oz. Chamomile Syrup (see recipe)

- 1 oz. coconut milk
- ½ oz. aquafaba

1. Place all of the ingredients in a cocktail shaker, fill it two-thirds of the way with ice, and shake until chilled.

2. Strain the cocktail into the coupe, garnish with chamomile blossoms and ground freeze-dried raspberries, and enjoy.

CHAMOMILE SYRUP: Add 1 tablespoon of chamomile blossoms or 2 bags of chamomile tea to a standard Simple Syrup (see page 20) after the sugar has dissolved. Let the syrup cool and strain before using or storing in the refrigerator.

TIME'S ARROW II

MIMINASHI
NAPA, CALIFORNIA

With Suntory and *Star Trek*'s help, here's a terrific play on a Negroni/Boulevardier from what was downtown Napa's popular izakaya, prepandemic; unfortunately, it is no longer.

GLASSWARE: **Rocks glass**
GARNISH: **Sesame & Citrus Candy (see page 388)**

- **1 oz. Sesame-Infused Whisky (see recipe)**
- **1 oz. Luxardo Bitter Bianco**

- **1 oz. Carpano Bianco Vermouth**
- **1 bar spoon Oleo Salis (see recipe)**

1. Place all of the ingredients in a mixing glass, fill it two-thirds of the way with ice, and stir until chilled.

2. Strain the cocktail over a large ice cube into the rocks glass, garnish with the Sesame & Citrus Candy, and enjoy.

SESAME-INFUSED WHISKY: Place 1 cup toasted sesame seeds and a 750 ml bottle of Suntory Toki whisky in a mason jar and let steep for 3 days. Strain before using or storing.

OLEO SALIS: Place the zest of 10 lemons and 10 oranges in a bowl, add ½ cup kosher salt, and, wearing latex gloves, work the mixture with your hands for 2 minutes. Cover and let the mixture sit overnight. Stir in 2 oz. Suntory Toki whisky and strain the liquid into a mason jar, pressing down on the solids to extract as much liquid as possible from them.

SESAME & CITRUS CANDY

You can cut the caramel into whatever shapes you like, but crosshatching in a simple rectangular pattern will yield the most usable pieces.

- ½ cup sugar
- 3 tablespoons toasted sesame seeds (mix of white and black)
- Zest of 1 lemon
- Zest of 1 orange
- ⅛ teaspoon baking soda
- 1 teaspoon Maldon sea salt

1. Line a baking sheet with parchment paper. Thinly coat a small saucepan with some of the sugar. Warm the sugar over medium-high heat and wait for it to begin melting. Gradually add more sugar to the spots in the pan where the sugar is liquefying. Once about a third of the sugar has been introduced, the pace of adding the sugar can be increased. When all of the sugar has been added, stir it with a wooden spoon until it has caramelized.

2. Add the sesame seeds, lemon zest, orange zest, and baking soda and stir until thoroughly combined.

3. Pour the mixture onto the parchment-lined baking sheet and use an offset spatula to spread the caramel in a thin layer.

4. While the caramel is still hot, sprinkle the salt over the surface. Let the caramel cool for 1 minute.

5. Use a sharp knife to score the firm, yet slightly tacky, caramel candy in whatever shapes you like.

6. Wait for the caramel to set fully before breaking it along the score marks.

BALI OLD FASHIONED

GOOSE & GANDER
ST. HELENA, CALIFORNIA

Many of the world's great cocktails were inspired by intrepid traveling bartenders. While Scott Beattie was traveling in Bali, Goose & Gander owner Andy Florsheim gave Beattie a call about opening the bar. Beattie came back to California with a giant stick of cinnamon and the idea for this take on an Old Fashioned, using a trio of spices to give the bourbon drink a whole new savory dimension.

GLASSWARE: Rocks glass
GARNISH: Orange slice

- **2 oz. St. George Breaking & Entering Bourbon**
- **¼ oz. Bali Spice Syrup (see recipe)**
- **Dash of Regan's Orange Bitters**
- **Dash of The Bitter Truth Orange Bitters**
- **Zest of 1 orange**

1. Place all of the ingredients, except for the orange zest, in a mixing glass, fill it two-thirds of the way with ice, and stir for 20 to 30 seconds.

2. Strain over one large ice cube into the rocks glass, express the orange zest over the cocktail, and discard the zest.

3. Garnish with the orange slice and enjoy.

BALI SPICE SYRUP: Break 9 inches of cinnamon sticks into small pieces. Add those pieces to a spice grinder along with 12 whole cloves and 12 star anise pods. Grind until the spices are fine, about 1 minute. Add the ground spices to a saucepan over medium heat and toast until they are aromatic, shaking the pan continually. Add 2 cups Simple Syrup (see page 20), bring to a boil, and then reduce the heat and simmer for 5 minutes. Turn off the heat and let the syrup cool for about 1 hour. Scrape the bottom of the pan to get all of the little seasoning bits and strain the syrup through a mesh strainer or chinois, using a spatula to help push the syrup through. Use immediately or store in the refrigerator.

NEGRONI CAFFE

GRANDMASTER RECORDS
LOS ANGELES, CALIFORNIA

Stevie Wonder, Foo Fighters, David Bowie—the list of artists who spent time in this space before it was converted into a restaurant and bar, with a stunning rooftop perch looking onto the Hollywood Hills, is staggering. And that musical mojo lingers in the décor and the rock 'n' roll attitude behind both the food and drinks menus.

GLASSWARE: Rocks glass
GARNISH: Strip of orange peel

- 1 oz. The Botanist Islay Dry Gin
- ½ oz. Espresso-Infused Campari (see recipe)
- ½ oz. sweet vermouth
- ¾ oz. Mr Black Coffee Liqueur
- Dash of Fee Brothers Aztec Chocolate Bitters

1. Place all of the ingredients in a cocktail shaker, fill it two-thirds of the way with ice, and shake until chilled.

2. Strain into the rocks glass, garnish with the strip of orange peel, and enjoy.

ESPRESSO-INFUSED CAMPARI: Place 2 tablespoons espresso beans and a 750 ml bottle of Campari in a large mason jar and let the mixture steep for 3 hours. Strain before using or storing.

TOMATO BEEF

VIRIDIAN
OAKLAND, CALIFORNIA

In early 2020, just before the COVID-19 pandemic struck the Bay Area, Viridian opened in Uptown Oakland with a giant wave of excitement. It's the rare high-energy/high-volume/high-quality cocktails establishment that is an effortlessly hip Hong Kong and '90s R & B scene.

The cocktail program is orchestrated by bar manager and Oakland native William Tsui (previously at Lazy Bear and Rich Table), who manages to make abstract ideas seem fully functional and drinkable in cocktail form, without the superfluous gaudy elements that many modern drinks tend to have. The cocktails are mesmerizing in terms of their flavor and purity—as you'll see when you taste this.

★

GLASSWARE: Rocks glass
GARNISH: Sprig of pink pepper

- 1¼ oz. tequila
- ¼ oz. basil eau de vie
- 1 oz. Tomato Water (see recipe)

- ½ oz. Pink Peppercorn Syrup (see recipe)
- ½ oz. fresh lime juice

1. Place all of the ingredients in a mixing glass, fill it two-thirds of the way with ice, and stir until chilled.

2. Strain the cocktail over ice into the rocks glass, garnish with the sprig of pink pepper, and enjoy.

TOMATO WATER: Place tomatoes in a blender, puree until smooth, and strain through a coffee filter.

PINK PEPPERCORN SYRUP: Place 3 cups sugar and 2 cups water in a saucepan and bring to a simmer, stirring to dissolve the sugar. Add 2 tablespoons pink peppercorns or 10 pink pepper sprigs to the syrup, simmer for 20 minutes, and strain. Let the syrup cool completely before using or storing.

BOURBON & SPICE

BARDO LOUNGE & SUPPER CLUB
OAKLAND, CALIFORNIA

Here's an autumnal leaning stirred bourbon cocktail from bar manager Brice Sanchez. Here's how assistant general manager Shannon Richey explains the drink: "Originally concocted as part of our seasonal cocktail menu, it's essentially a wintery take on a classic Old Fashioned. With the addition of sweet, herbaceous Montenegro, and spiced pear liqueur from St. George, one of our favorite local distilleries, the Bourbon & Spice is everything nice. Finished with house-made fire bitters, which have been infused with mulling spices and chiles, this drink will keep you warm all winter long."

GLASSWARE: Rocks glass
GARNISH: Strip of orange peel

- **1 oz. Bulleit Bourbon**
- **½ oz. Amaro Montenegro**
- **½ oz. St. George Spiced Pear Liqueur**
- **Dash of Regan's Orange Bitters**
- **Dash of Bittermens Hellfire Habanero Shrub**
- **½ teaspoon Demerara Syrup (see page 63)**

1. Place all of the ingredients in a mixing glass, fill it two-thirds of the way with ice, and stir until chilled.

2. Strain the cocktail over a large ice cube into the rocks glass, express the strip of orange peel over the cocktail, garnish the drink with it, and enjoy.

THE TOUGH GET GOING

JUANITA & MAUDE
ALBANY, CALIFORNIA

The quiet city of Albany, Berkeley's neighbor to the north, is home to this ideal farm-to-table, friendly neighborhood/special occasion spot from chef/owner Scott Eastman and owner/designer Ariane Owens. General manager/bar and wine director Nicholas Danielson is the talented mind behind the noteworthy cocktail menu with many consistent highlights, like this take on the East Bay's own classic, the Mai Tai.

GLASSWARE: Large tumbler
GLASSWARE: Strip of orange peel

- 1½ oz. Royal Standard Dry Rum
- ½ oz. fresh orange juice
- ½ oz. Orgeat (see page 50)
- ½ oz. Pierre Ferrand Dry Curaçao
- ¼ oz. fresh lime juice
- ½ oz. Ron Abuelo 12-Year-Old Rum

1. Place all of the ingredients, except for the Ron Abuelo rum, in a cocktail shaker, fill it two-thirds of the way with ice, and shake until chilled.

2. Fill the large tumbler with crushed ice and strain the cocktail over it.

3. Float the Ron Abuelo rum on top of the cocktail, pouring it over the back of a spoon.

4. Garnish with the strip of orange peel and enjoy.

OH, WHAT'S THAT?

With a coupe that looks a teacup, guests are always asking, "Oh, what's that?" In response, Here and Now renamed their take on the Espresso Martini.

★

GLASSWARE: Coupe
GARNISH: 3 espresso beans

- 2 oz. Argonaut Saloon Strength Brandy
- 1 oz. brewed espresso

- ½ oz. Mr Black Coffee Liqueur
- ½ oz. Simple Syrup (see page 20)

1. Place all of the ingredients in a cocktail shaker, fill it two-thirds of the way with ice, and shake until chilled.

2. Double-strain into the coupe, garnish with the espresso beans, and enjoy.

RABO DE GALO

BOSSA NOVA
LOS ANGELES, CALIFORNIA

Bartender Robbie Reza's Rabo de Galo is a take on the traditional Brazilian cocktail that connects the sweet and fruity flavor of Don Papa Rum with the texture and nuttiness of a cashew.

GLASSWARE: Rocks glass
GARNISH: Orange twist

- 1½ oz. Don Papa Rum
- ½ oz. sweet vermouth
- ¾ oz. Lo-Fi Dry Vermouth
- ½ oz. Cashew Syrup (see recipe)
- 2 dashes of Angostura Bitters

1. Place all of the ingredients in a cocktail shaker, fill it two-thirds of the way with ice, and shake until chilled.

2. Strain over a large ice cube into the rocks glass, garnish with the orange twist, and enjoy.

CASHEW SYRUP: Preheat the oven to 350°F. Place 1 cup cashews on a baking sheet, place them in the oven, and toast for 5 minutes. Remove the cashews from the oven and set them aside. Place 1 cup sugar and 1 cup water in a saucepan and bring to a boil, stirring to dissolve the sugar. Place the syrup and cashews in a blender and puree until smooth. Strain the syrup and let it cool completely before using or storing.

MR. COCO

Originally created at a dinner party in Las Vegas for an iconic personality and his billionaire friends, and inspired by a Scottish Westie, this exquisite alternative to a Piña Colada is this high-end bar's signature drink.

GLASSWARE: Rocks glass
GARNISH: None

- 1½ oz. Cîroc Coconut Vodka
- ¾ oz. Plantation XO 20th Anniversary Rum
- ¾ oz. Organic Mixology Coconut & Lychee Liqueur
- 2 oz. Liquid Alchemist Coconut Syrup
- ½ oz. fresh lemon juice
- 3 spritzes of Luxardo Amaretto & Angostura House Mix, to top (see recipe)

1. Place all of the ingredients, except for the house mix, in a cocktail shaker, fill it two-thirds of the way with ice, and shake until chilled.

2. Strain the cocktail over ice into the rocks glass, spritz with the house mix, and enjoy.

LUXARDO AMARETTO & ANGOSTURA HOUSE MIX: Combine ¾ oz. Luxardo Amaretto with ¼ oz. Angostura Bitters and place the mixture in a spray bottle.

EXCHANGE STUDENT

NOSTALGIA BAR AND LOUNGE
LOS ANGELES, CALIFORNIA

A sole French element amidst a host of Italian ingredients, the Lillet proves to be a quick study here.

GLASSWARE: Rocks glass
GARNISH: None

- Black lava salt, for the rim
- 1 oz. Cynar 70
- 1 oz. Punt e Mes
- ¾ oz. Cucumber-Infused Campari (see recipe)
- ½ oz. Lillet
- ¼ oz. Luxardo maraschino liqueur

1. Wet the rim of the rocks glass and coat half of it with the black lava salt. Add a large ice cube to the rimmed glass.

2. Place all of the ingredients in a mixing glass, fill it two-thirds of the way with ice, and stir until chilled.

3. Strain the cocktail into the rimmed glass and enjoy.

CUCUMBER-INFUSED CAMPARI: Peel and chop 1 large cucumber and place it in a large mason jar. Add 4 cups Campari and steep in a cool, dark place for 1 week. Strain before using or storing.

THREE WISHES

This rooftop bar in Burbank offers expansive views and wonderful drinks. The bar's design is inspired by the "greenrooms" where celebs and other Hollywood folk relax before and after shows and appearances, which explains why the menu draws from popular movies, ranging from *Grease* to *Fight Club* and, in the case of Three Wishes, *Aladdin*.

★

GLASSWARE: Teacups
GARNISH: Bachelor's buttons

- 2 oz. brewed jasmine tea
- 2 oz. honey
- 3 red seedless grapes
- 1 oz. fresh lemon juice
- 1 oz. red wine
- 4 oz. Monkey 47 Schwarzwald Dry Gin
- Dry ice, as needed

1. Combine the tea and honey and stir until the mixture is syrupy.

2. Place the grapes in a cocktail shaker and muddle. Add the tea mixture, lemon juice, and red wine and dry shake for 15 seconds.

3. Place the gin a separate cocktail shaker, fill it two-thirds of the way with ice, and shake until chilled.

4. Strain the gin over large ice cubes into the teacups.

5. Add dry ice to a tea infuser and place that in a teapot. Add the muddled mixture, which will create "smoke." Pour the mixture in the teapot into the teacups, garnish with bachelor's buttons, and enjoy.

FLOR DE LA PIÑA

CHICA
LAS VEGAS, NEVADA

A fruity cocktail with a spicy kick. The Hibiscus & Habanero Syrup is a quick and easy way to incorporate brilliant color and additional punch.

GLASSWARE: Rocks glass
GARNISH: Hibiscus blossom, fresh sage leaf

- 1½ oz. Espolòn Tequila
- ¾ oz. fresh lime juice
- ½ oz. Hibiscus & Habanero Syrup (see recipe)
- 1 oz. pineapple juice
- 3 fresh sage leaves
- Dash of orange bitters

1. Place all of the ingredients in a cocktail shaker, fill it two-thirds of the way with ice, and shake until chilled.

2. Strain the cocktail over ice into the rocks glass, garnish with the hibiscus blossom and fresh sage, and enjoy.

HIBISCUS & HABANERO SYRUP: In a large saucepan, combine 3 halved habanero peppers with ½ lb. dried hibiscus blossoms, 2 quarts sugar, and 4 quarts water and bring to a boil. Once boiling, reduce the heat and simmer for 30 minutes. Remove the pan from heat, strain the syrup, and let it cool completely before using or storing.

DISGRUNTLED MAI TAI

ELECTRA COCKTAIL CLUB
LAS VEGAS, NEVADA

Ah, nothing says Vegas like a tasty mash-up of appropriated Tahitian traditions and a boozy, anise-flavored German digestif (Underberg).

★

GLASSWARE: Rocks glass
GARNISH: Fresh mint, cocktail umbrella

- 1 oz. Smith & Cross Rum
- 1 oz. Aperol
- 1 oz. fresh lime juice
- ½ oz. Orgeat (see page 50)
- ½ oz. curaçao
- Miniature bottle of Underberg

1. Place all of the ingredients, except for the Underberg, in a cocktail shaker, fill it two-thirds of the way with ice, and shake until chilled.

2. Fill the rocks glass with crushed ice and strain the cocktail over it.

3. Carefully flip the bottle of Underberg into the cocktail so it is upside-down, garnish with fresh mint and the cocktail umbrella, and enjoy.

NORTHWEST

Avocado Daiquiri ★ Ghost in the Shell

Mojito de Piña ★ Berries & Bubbles

American Troubadour ★ Sleeping Lotus

Hurricane Drops ★ El Nacional

A la Louisiane ★ Secret Life of Plants

Lychee Thieves ★ The Power of One

Hijinks ★ East of Eden

Bloody Scandi ★ Ox Blood Cocktail

Bamboo ★ Goodnight, Moon

Two-Tailed Fox ★ Ame Soeur

62 Panorama Punch

The final stop on our tour is more than capable of providing a suitable finish for such a memorable trip.

While Brooklyn is the place most people will think of when asked which city transformed the American culinary scene and shifted it toward craft and a focus on local ingredients, in truth, Seattle and Portland, Oregon, should probably be given priority in that discussion. First, there is the Northwest's ample rainfall and temperate climate to consider, two qualities that pair to foster one of the world's great agricultural regions. Second, there is the fact that Portland's insistence on all things artisanal was powerful enough to sustain a satirical sketch show for eight seasons.

The mixology in both spots more than kept pace with the local move toward local, craft, and quality. In Portland, Lucy Brennan laid the groundwork for a cocktail scene that can trade blows with cities five times its size. In Seattle, Murray Stenson inspired an entire generation of bartenders and helped Seattle smoothly transition from sleepy fishing village to global mover and shaker. It may the end of the continent, but it is obvious that things are just getting started in the Pacific Northwest's big cities.

AVOCADO DAIQUIRI

CREATED BY LUCY BRENNAN
PORTLAND, OREGON

Portland bartending legend Lucy Brennan has two methods of creating the signature Lemon-Lime Juice that appears in most of her cocktails. The recipe included here is the less labor-intensive version. Brennan recommends pairing this drink with a burger or spicy ceviche.

GLASSWARE: Cocktail glass
GARNISH: Pomegranate concentrate

- 2 oz. Bacardí Superior Rum
- 2 oz. aged rum
- Flesh from ¼ medium-ripe avocado
- ½ oz. half-and-half
- ¼ oz. Lemon-Lime Juice (see recipe)
- 2 oz. Simple Syrup (see page 20)

1. Place all of the ingredients in a blender, add 1½ cups ice, and blend until the mixture is silky smooth with no trace of ice—the consistency of the drink should be similar to heavy cream.

2. Pour the cocktail into the wineglass and gently drizzle the pomegranate concentrate over the top. Place a cocktail straw or toothpick at the top of the zigzag pattern, pull through the center of the pomegranate concentrate to make a series of hearts, and enjoy.

LEMON-LIME JUICE: Place 1 (16 oz.) bottle of Santa Cruz 100% lime juice and 1 (16 oz.) bottle of Santa Cruz 100% lemon juice in a large container and shake to combine. Use immediately or store in the refrigerator.

Q & A WITH LUCY BRENNAN

Lucy Brennan seems to be synonymous with cocktail culture in Portland. In fact, the esteemed Jeffrey Morgenthaler insists that she essentially created cocktail culture in Portland. Brennan has worked at various area bars and restaurants and even has her own book of cocktail recipes.

How did you become interested in cocktails in the first place?

I think because I was fortunate enough to start working at Saucebox downtown. So I opened that bar with Bruce Carey, who used to be the owner. I started off as a bartender and then after a couple of months I became the bar manager and really got free rein to be creative and to come up with some really fun cocktails. This was the mid-1990s. That's how I got into it, and that's how I was able to be creative, and not have the requirements of making basic cocktails. Not that there's anything wrong with that.

How do you think Portland's cocktail scene has evolved over the years?

Well, since I've been bartending in Portland, since 1995, I think Portland was one of the first cities in the nation to start the cocktail revolution. I shouldn't say started, but be part of it. It was really fun to watch every restaurant have their own craft cocktail menu available, which was new, so that was really fun. I think it went through a period of being a bit overambitious. I've never been a fan of the term "mixologist." I'm a bartender. At that time, I had my own restaurant and just kind of kept my head down. I would go to Tales of the Cocktail in New Orleans. And that was really fun because that's when it was getting its own momentum—dissecting the bartending. Before that, people just bartended to get through college. It's different now; people look at it differently.

What do you think was the beginning of cocktails in Portland?

Before Saucebox opened, in 1995, a couple of places that aren't around anymore were doing fantastic cocktails. One place was Brazen Bean, that was in northwest Portland, and then it was Zefiro, and I worked at Zefiro because Bruce also owned that. And that was definitely, you know, again, bridging the kitchen and the bar. Making simple syrups, making different kinds of purees, and tapping into the whole farmers market scene. That evolved the bar too, that program. So as far as when did it start, I would have to say early 1990s.

What do you think makes Portland's bar scene unique compared to other cities?

Well, I don't know if that's the case anymore, because I feel like everyone has really come up to speed. I feel like the farmers market is in every city, and like every little district within the city, and that has a huge impact. I think the public has really wanted to become educated when it comes to spirits. You've got all the small distilleries and the microbreweries. So it really unfolded naturally. I don't know where we're at now, considering the last two years of the pandemic. It's nice to see people go back out and enjoy really well-thought-out drinks that aren't ambitious.

Any favorite stories from your time behind the bar?

Laughs Well, what kind of stories? You mean, drinkwise?

What's the worst order you've ever gotten?

Oh my gosh, no, you can't ask me that. I think it was in the 1990s, someone ordered a single malt scotch with Diet Coke. I was like, "Hell no, I'm not going to put those together." But I guess the funniest story for me behind the bar is when I came up with this drink called the Avocado Daiquiri (see page 416). Basically, it was guacamole in a glass. It was disgusting. My friends thought I was nuts. It took years to perfect. It became one of those ugly ducklings that becomes a swan. As far as customers having impressions on me, um, they're all wonderful.

What's your favorite cocktail to make personally?

It depends. In the winter, I really enjoy Black Manhattans. In the summer, you know, a really good Last Word or Gimlet. Really simple and clean. And you think they would be easy to make, but it's one of those things. It's kind of like if you go in and order someone's Daiquiri. It's a telltale sign if a bartender can make those drinks really, really well. I really like the Hugo Spritz. It's not an Aperol Spritz, but you drink it at the same time. You know, the happy hour, the aperitif hour in Italy.

What is essential for novice cocktail makers to have in their home bars? Do you think there's any essential equipment or essential ingredients?

Definitely bitters. Definitely a good mixing glass. Good ice. As far as equipment, those are the items I want to have. As far as the products to have at home in order to make basic drinks? A really well-made bourbon, an elegant gin, a handsome vodka, a fun tequila.

What else?

Those would be the four I start with.

When I was in Las Vegas recently, I saw an automated cocktail bar where people could order drinks and a machine would make them. Do you think machines will eventually replace bartenders?

Bartenders are always going to be around. It's one of the oldest crafts. Especially now, coming out of COVID, when people want that interaction. They work in Vegas, they may have that demand, but definitely a no. A hard no.

What's your process for creating cocktails? How do you start usually?

It depends on what I'm doing and what spirit I'm using. I always blind taste myself on the spirit. What I mean by that is that I smell it. I get the notes—similar to wine tasting. See what I get from it. And then see how I can build on it without overpowering it. For me, you really want to showcase the spirit. You want to elevate. Some people put too many ingredients in, and for me, I want to keep it below five. Five is the maximum probably. Four ingredients to a cocktail I think is really smart.

Is there one absolute no-no in cocktail making?

Oh, no, not off the top of my head. Nope. When I said about the bartending scene becoming too ambitious, that's what I meant. Too many ingredients.

And what do you think makes a drink more culinary? How can people elevate their cocktails at home without overcomplicating them?

If you go to the farmers market, and you have something you really like, like apricots or what's in season right now. Take those and you can make your own infusions. You can make an Apricot Martini or something really simple. Not something over-the-top with like 18 ingredients in it, where you're like, "Oh, there's tequila in that." Your drink should be well-balanced. Flavorful, approachable, and well-balanced.

GHOST IN THE SHELL

CREATED BY CUYLER HARRIS
SEATTLE, WASHINGTON

" I made this one when I was the bar manager of Brunswick & Hunt up in Ballard between 2015 and 2019, a cute little family-owned bar with a restaurant attached. I had carte blanche over the whole menu and always rotated seasonal stuff in and out. I was able to play with a lot of beautiful ingredients and really stretch my legs, creatively speaking. This is easily one of the most popular cocktails I ever created and it became a mainstay on the menu year-round. It's spicy and refreshing, with a hint of nutty, sweet smoke and a big herbaceous backbone."—Cuyler Harris

GLASSWARE: Collins glass

GARNISH: Fresh mint

- 1 oz. Del Maguey Vida Mezcal
- 1 oz. amontillado sherry
- ¾ oz. fresh lime juice
- ½ oz. Orgeat (see page 50)
- ½ oz. Ginger Syrup (see page 129)

1. Place all of the ingredients in a cocktail shaker, fill it two-thirds of the way with ice, and shake until chilled.

2. Fill the Collins glass with crushed ice and double-strain the cocktail over it.

3. Top with more crushed ice, garnish with fresh mint, and enjoy.

MOJITO DE PIÑA

ANDINA
PORTLAND, OREGON

If you are in Portland, Andina is a must, serving Peruvian food and cocktails that will be burned into your brain for years.

GLASSWARE: Rocks glass
GARNISH: None

- 1½ oz. Pineapple-Infused Rum (see recipe)
- 1 oz. fresh lime juice
- 1 oz. pineapple puree
- 5 fresh basil leaves, torn in half
- 1½ tablespoons caster (superfine) sugar
- 1 oz. ice water

1. Place all of the ingredients in a cocktail shaker, fill it two-thirds of the way with ice, and shake vigorously until chilled.

2. Pour the contents of the shaker into the rocks glass and enjoy.

PINEAPPLE-INFUSED RUM: Place 10½ oz. chopped pineapple and a 750 ml bottle of rum in a mason jar and steep for 1 week. Strain before using or storing at room temperature.

BERRIES & BUBBLES

CREATED BY KATHY CASEY
SEATTLE, WASHINGTON

"This cocktail celebrates lush Pacific Northwest raspberries, which, when in season, have an intoxicating flavor and aroma. You can find flower ice cube molds online."—Kathy Casey

GLASSWARE: Coupe
GARNISH: Edible flower blossoms or fresh raspberry

- **3 to 4 fresh raspberries**
- **1½ oz. vodka or gin**
- **½ oz. Simple Syrup (see page 20)**
- **½ oz. fresh lemon juice**
- **1½ oz. Champagne or sparkling Rosé**

1. Chill the coupe in the freezer.
2. Place all of the ingredients, except for the Champagne, in a cocktail shaker, fill it two-thirds of the way with ice, and shake until chilled.
3. Double-strain the cocktail into the chilled coupe.
4. Top with the Champagne, garnish with edible flower blossoms or a raspberry, and enjoy.

AMERICAN TROUBADOUR

CEREUS PDX
PORTLAND, OREGON

Cereus attempts to make their cocktails both exciting and balanced. They have achieved their goal with this one, thanks in great part to the reverse dry shake. With reverse dry shaking, you first shake everything with ice and then strain everything and shake again without ice before serving. Be careful! There is no suction during dry shaking and this can leave you with a real mess. Hold down the shaker top tightly to avoid any issues.

GLASSWARE: Collins glass
GARNISH: Fresh mint, freshly grated nutmeg, strip of orange peel

- 1 oz. Wild Turkey 81 Bourbon
- ½ oz. Fernet-Branca Menta
- ½ oz. Grand Marnier
- 1 oz. nitro cold brew
- ¼ oz. Demerara Syrup (see page 63)
- 2 dashes of 18.21 Japanese Chili Lime Bitters

1. Place all of the ingredients in a cocktail shaker, fill it two-thirds of the way with ice, and shake until chilled.

2. Strain, discard the ice in the shaker, and return the cocktail to the shaker. Dry shake for 10 seconds.

3. Pour the cocktail over ice into the Collins glass, garnish with fresh mint, freshly grated nutmeg, and the strip of orange peel, and enjoy.

SLEEPING LOTUS

HALE PELE
PORTLAND, OREGON

Nestled between a doughnut shop and a fireplace store on NE Broadway, Hale Pele is a tiny little tiki bar that provides an outsized experience for all five senses.

GLASSWARE: Collins glass
GARNISH: Fresh mint, edible flower blossom

- 3 fresh mint leaves
- 2 oz. gin
- 1 oz. Orgeat (see page 50)
- ¾ oz. fresh lemon juice
- 2 dashes of orange bitters

1. Place the mint in a cocktail shaker and muddle.

2. Add ice and the remaining ingredients and shake until chilled.

3. Fill the Collins glass with crushed ice and double-strain the cocktail over it.

4. Garnish with fresh mint and the edible flower blossom and enjoy.

HURRICANE DROPS

HALE PELE
PORTLAND, OREGON

Mixing tropical fruits with gin, ginger, and rum produces a serve that deserves just one adjective: delightful.

★

GLASSWARE: Collins glass
GARNISH: 3 pineapple leaves, edible orchid

- 1 oz. Plantation 3 Stars Rum
- ½ oz. gin
- ¾ oz. fresh lemon juice
- 1 oz. pineapple juice
- 1 oz. guava puree
- ¾ oz. Ginger Syrup (see page 129)
- 1 bar spoon Herbsaint
- 4 dashes of Angostura Bitters

1. Place all of the ingredients, except for the bitters, in a mixing glass, add 2 oz. crushed ice, and stir until foamy.

2. Pour the contents of the mixing glass into the Collins glass, add the bitters, and top with more crushed ice.

3. Garnish with the pineapple leaves and edible orchid and enjoy.

EL NACIONAL

Mezcal and mole are a natural pairing that is complexly enhanced by the earthiness of the Ardbeg.

★

GLASSWARE: Coupe
GARNISH: Lemon twist

- 1 oz. Del Maguey Vida Mezcal
- 1 oz. Campari
- ½ oz. Luxardo Amaro Abano
- ½ oz. dry vermouth

- 3 dashes of Bittermens Xocolatl Mole Bitters
- Spritz of Ardbeg 5-Year Islay Scotch Whisky, to top

1. Place all of the ingredients, except for the Ardbeg, in a mixing glass, fill it two-thirds of the way with ice, and stir until chilled.

2. Strain the cocktail into the coupe and spritz it with the Ardbeg.

3. Garnish with the lemon twist and enjoy.

A LA LOUISIANE

A mid-century modern lounge and cocktail bar within the Hotel deLuxe, the Driftwood Room is expert at turning out cocktails that feel both timeless and contemporary.

GLASSWARE: Coupe

GARNISH: Fabbri Amarena Cherry

- 1¾ oz. rye whiskey
- ¾ oz. sweet vermouth
- ¼ oz. Bénédictine
- 3 dashes of absinthe
- 3 dashes of Peychaud's Bitters

1. Chill the coupe in the freezer.

2. Place all of the ingredients in a mixing glass, fill it two-thirds of the way with ice, and stir until chilled.

3. Strain the cocktail into the chilled coupe, garnish with the Fabbri Amarena Cherry, and enjoy.

SECRET LIFE OF PLANTS

HEY LOVE
PORTLAND, OREGON

Hey Love is a true wonder, having managed to create a tropical paradise inside, complete with cocktails to carry on that theme.

★

GLASSWARE: Tumbler

GARNISH: Fresh Thai basil

- 1½ oz. lightly aged rum
- ¾ oz. Mango & Oolong Syrup (see recipe)
- ¾ oz. fresh lime juice
- ¼ oz. Orgeat (see page 50)
- ¼ oz. falernum
- 10 drops of 10 Percent Saline Solution (see page 313)
- Dash of absinthe

1. Place all of the ingredients in a cocktail shaker, fill it two-thirds of the way with ice, and shake until chilled.

2. Fill the tumbler with crushed ice and strain the cocktail over it.

3. Top with more crushed ice, garnish with the fresh Thai basil, and enjoy.

MANGO & OOLONG SYRUP: Place ¾ cup water in a saucepan and heat it to 195°F. Add ¼ cup loose-leaf oolong tea and steep for 5 minutes. Strain the tea, discard the leaves, and return the tea to the saucepan. Add 30 oz. mango puree, 30 oz. white sugar, 1 (12 oz.) can of mango nectar, and a scant 2½ teaspoons citric acid (12 grams) and warm the mixture over low heat, stirring to dissolve the sugar. When the syrup is well combined, remove the pan from heat and let it cool completely before using or storing.

LYCHEE THIEVES

RUMBA
SEATTLE, WASHINGTON

Colorful, fragrant, fresh—this drink is the tropics in a glass.

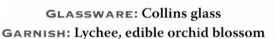

GLASSWARE: Collins glass
GARNISH: Lychee, edible orchid blossom

- ¾ oz. Rhum J.M Agricole Blanc 55% Rhum
- ¾ oz. Byrrh Grand Quinquina
- ¾ oz. Giffard Lichi-Li
- ¾ oz. fresh lime juice
- ¼ oz. Rich Simple Syrup (see page 247)
- 1½ oz. ginger beer, to top

1. Place all of the ingredients, except for the ginger beer, in a cocktail shaker, fill it two-thirds of the way with ice, and shake until chilled.

2. Strain the cocktail over ice into the Collins glass and top with the ginger beer.

3. Garnish with the lychee and orchid blossom and enjoy.

THE POWER OF ONE

QUAINTRELLE
PORTLAND, OREGON

A quaintrelle is a woman who emphasizes a life of passion, expressed through personal style, leisurely pastimes, charm, and a cultivation of life's pleasures. This cocktail from Camille Cavan feels like it comes from someone who checks all of those boxes, and wants to teach others to do the same.

GLASSWARE: Collins glass
GARNISH: 1 teaspoon shaved fresh ginger

- **2 oz. Appleton Estate Reserve Blend Rum**
- **1 oz. coconut milk**
- **1 oz. fresh lime juice**
- **1 oz. Demerara Syrup (see page 63)**

1. Place all of the ingredients in a cocktail shaker, fill it two-thirds of the way with ice, and shake until chilled.

2. Fill the Collins glass with crushed ice and strain the cocktail over it.

3. Top with more crushed ice, garnish with the shaved fresh ginger, and enjoy.

HIJINKS

"**S**ingle malt Scotch drinkers seem to rarely mix their whiskey, so this cocktail is a little nod to showing them that they can relax a bit and have some fun with it. No need to be so serious! The delicate floral aromas from the chamomile and fino sherry really help to create a unique flavor profile that is definitely nontraditional of single malt Scotch cocktails." —Jesse Cyr

GLASSWARE: Coupe
GARNISH: Dehydrated lemon wheel

- 1½ oz. Glenmorangie X Scotch Whisky
- ¾ oz. Lustau Fino Sherry
- ¾ oz. Chamomile Syrup (see page 385)
- ½ oz. fresh lemon juice

1. Place all of the ingredients in a cocktail shaker, fill it two-thirds of the way with ice, and shake until chilled.

2. Strain the cocktail into the coupe, garnish with the dehydrated lemon wheel, and enjoy.

EAST OF EDEN

BIBLE CLUB
PORTLAND, OREGON

A creamy, floral, delicately sweet, and bright cocktail that tastes like an elegant, lavender-infused Piña Colada.

★

GLASSWARE: Coupe
GARNISH: None

- 1½ oz. vodka
- ½ oz. coconut rum
- ¼ oz. heavy cream
- ½ oz. egg white
- ½ oz. fresh lemon juice
- ½ oz. Simple Syrup (see page 20)
- 2 dashes of lavender bitters

1. Place all of the ingredients in a cocktail shaker, fill it two-thirds of the way with ice, and shake until chilled.

2. Strain the cocktail into the coupe and enjoy.

MURRAY STENSON

Every successful bar owner in Seattle identifies Murray Stenson as the godfather of the local cocktail scene, and many of them credit Murray as their own personal inspiration as well. All consider it a privilege to sit at his bar. He combines encyclopedic knowledge with a jovial approach and a focus on service to form the perfect bar persona.

"I was never one of the cool kids in school," Murray said. The iconic barman learned the craft of hospitality and the art of conversation, you see—they were not natural gifts. "I was afforded the potential to learn about drinking very gradually. At that time, the accent was on taking care of the customer. Hospitality was the number-one thing, making the customer happy." He wonders aloud if that is still the case.

Starting his career behind the service well at Benjamins, Murray trained himself in the essentials of bartending—proper pouring and shaking, efficiency of movement, and the fluidity of presentation. When he was thrown in front of guests for the first time at Henry's, he practiced his showmanship and dialogue until the shy caterpillar transformed into the bright butterfly he is today. He hit his stride and discovered his aptitude for the craft. "The reason I got into bartending," he explains, "is so I could hang out with all the cool adults, smoking and drinking. I could hang out with those people and get paid for it." He was hooked, and the sky was the limit.

"After a couple of years, I told one of my regular bar guests I'm going to stick with this and asked, 'Who are the best bartenders in town?'" The regular named some of his favorite barkeeps around the city. "I would post up at their bars and learn the basics. I was fortunate, at that time in America, drinking was at a nadir. Everyone was doing drugs instead."

It was a very different time, indeed. When he started work at the Carousel Room at Oliver's in 1978, it was the first cocktail bar in the entire state with windows—decency at the time required drinkers to go about their business away from public view. The city also enforced morality by forbidding the sale of packaged alcoholic beverages on Sundays. "In those days," Murray explains, "if you were a woman and unescorted, you could not sit at the bar by yourself. It was really primeval." (His time at Oliver's was not absent of fun, however; one evening he had to cut off an intoxicated guest, and when Murray removed the man's drink, it came to fisticuffs).

Murray worked stints of differing lengths at bars around Seattle through the 1980s, following the money. When he wasn't being quizzed by his bartender disciples, he was getting job offers from restaurant owners who wanted to steal Murray and his legion of followers. Wherever he went, success seemed to follow. "One of the highlights of my 40-plus years of bartending was one night working with Jim Luby," the man Murray credits as the best bartender he ever worked with. "We had a full bar, and two deuces [two groups of two people] walked in, and the manager told these people that he could seat them in the dining room for drinks, while they waited for dinner at the bar." Murray erupts with laughter. "That was the best job I ever had."

ZIG ZAG, THE COCKTAIL RENAISSANCE, AND TODAY

Murray feels that the essence of Zig Zag Cafe, what makes it special, is the ambience. The inviting atmosphere is what draws people in and makes them want to stay. "It amazes me how cozy and warm it is," he says. After Murray spent all of the 1990s inspiring a new generation of bartenders at Il Bistro, Ben Dougherty was finally able to poach Murray and bring him to Zig Zag in 2001, the bar at which he would spend the next decade of his storied career. "The community was close-knit—exclusive membership, up until the 2000s," he remembers. "Then it exploded."

As a cocktail celebrity of sorts, Murray's employment is the ultimate endorsement of a Seattle bar, and Zig Zag was soon packed with his loyal regulars. When the national cocktail renaissance blossomed in 2005, Zig Zag was positioned as the epicenter of it all; soon, a line would gather at the entrance before they opened. It was like the Beatles playing on *Ed Sullivan*, but for cocktail nerds. "I had a lot of customers from those early days say that they miss that era," Murray says. It seems like a good place, toward the end of our chat, to ask his thoughts on the current cocktail scene, the latest generation of bartenders, and how the industry differs today from his start in the 1970s.

"The hospitality has suffered," he laments. "I think a lot of that has gone away, it's something that I have been saying for 20 years. The professionalism of bartenders has increased—their recipes and their methodology. That has been spectacular to a fault." He pauses to choose his next words. "There is...a lot of cocktail snobbery that I really hate.

"It grieves me," Murray continues, "that this new generation of bartenders has no experience with hospitality. I had a longtime regular bar guest—since 1990—who went to a bar here in town that had a real hotshot national reputation. He sits at this guy's bar, where the previous customer had spilled water on the countertop." The bartender took his order, served his drink, and never once cleaned the bar. "You have to consider how people are feeling," he says with the certainty of a professor. "You have to read the moment. Hospitality is everything. Focus on what the customer is looking for, what the customer is feeling."

BLOODY SCANDI

CREATED BY KATHY CASEY
SEATTLE, WASHINGTON

Seattle bartending legend Kathy Casey talks you through this creation of hers: "Inspired by a trip to Portland, I combined House Spirits Aquavit with Demitri's Bloody Mary Seasoning (a favorite bar staple from my longtime friend Demitri Pallis), a pinch of fresh dill, and tomato juice, and garnished it up with all my favorite pickled things. As a Scandinavian, I personally would skewer some pickled herring too. If you prefer less aquavit in your drink, try substituting half of it for your favorite vodka."

GLASSWARE: Collins glass
GARNISH: Pickled beets, pickled cucumber spear,
other pickled vegetables (if desired), fresh dill

- 1½ oz. House Spirits Aquavit
- ¾ oz. Demitri's Extra Horseradish Bloody Mary Seasoning
- 4 oz. tomato juice
- Pinch of chopped fresh dill

1. Build the cocktail in the Collins glass, adding the ingredients in the order they are listed.

2. Fill the glass with ice and stir until chilled.

3. Garnish with pickled beets, the pickled cucumber spear, other pickled vegetables (if desired), and fresh dill and enjoy.

OX BLOOD COCKTAIL

OX RESTAURANT
PORTLAND, OREGON

★

This recipe was featured in OX's 2016 cookbook, *Around the Fire*, by Greg Denton and Gabrielle Quiñónez Denton, with Stacy Adimando.

★

GLASSWARE: Rocks glass
GARNISH: Fresh tarragon

- 1½ oz. bourbon
- 1 oz. Beet Syrup (see recipe)
- ¾ oz. fresh lemon juice
- Pinch of kosher salt

1. Place all of the ingredients in a cocktail shaker, fill it two-thirds of the way with ice, and shake until chilled.

2. Double-strain over ice into the rocks glass, garnish with fresh tarragon, and enjoy.

BEET SYRUP: In a small saucepan, combine 1 cup freshly pressed beet juice and ⅓ cup cane sugar and bring to a simmer over medium heat, stirring to dissolve the sugar. Remove the pan from heat and let the syrup cool completely before using or storing in the refrigerator.

BAMBOO

FAIRMONT OLYMPIC HOTEL
SEATTLE, WASHINGTON

The creator of the Bamboo, Jesse Cyr, says it's "a great cocktail option for when you want to drink, but also want to take it easy. Just because you want a low-ABV beverage doesn't mean you need to make a sacrifice when it comes to flavor. The sherry blend in this Bamboo is key to achieving a great depth and complexity."

GLASSWARE: Collins glass
GARNISH: Fresh mint

- 1½ oz. dry vermouth
- ¾ oz. amontillado sherry
- ½ oz. fino sherry
- ¼ oz. Lustau East India Solera Sherry
- 1 bar spoon Simple Syrup (see page 20)
- 2 dashes of Angostura Bitters
- 2 dashes of orange bitters

1. Chill the Collins glass in the freezer.
2. Place all of the ingredients in a mixing glass, fill it two-thirds of the way with ice, and stir until chilled.
3. Strain the cocktail over ice into the chilled glass, garnish with the fresh mint, and enjoy.

GOODNIGHT, MOON

TEARDROP LOUNGE
PORTLAND, OREGON

An extraordinary cocktail that seems both like some magical potion from the ancient world and on the cutting edge of modern mixology.

★

GLASSWARE: Collins glass
GARNISH: None

- 1 oz. Pommeau de Normandie
- ½ oz. heavy cream
- 2½ oz. Fennel & Walnut Syrup (see recipe)
- 1 oz. club soda

1. Add ice to the Collins glass and build the drink in the glass, adding the ingredients in the order they are listed.

2. Stir until chilled and enjoy.

FENNEL & WALNUT SYRUP: Place equal parts maple-walnut syrup and freshly pressed fennel juice in a mason jar, stir well, and use as desired.

TWO-TAILED FOX

CREATED BY CUYLER HARRIS
SEATTLE, WASHINGTON

66 **I** wanted to create something that was refreshing enough to be enjoyed on a hot summer day, but also something spirit-forward that could be sipped slowly and wasn't the same old tall, fruit-juice refresher, Margarita, or Daiquiri riff that one might see on a typical menu. Not a lot of people may know how perfect of a pairing of allspice and brandy can be, but I think that's one of the key elements to this drink."—Cuyler Harris

GLASSWARE: Double rocks glass

GARNISH: Dehydrated lime wheel

- 1½ oz. Singani 63 Bolivian Brandy
- ¾ oz. Dolin Blanc
- ¼ oz. Pierre Ferrand Dry Curaçao
- ¼ oz. Del Maguey Vida Mezcal
- ¼ oz. St. Elizabeth Allspice Dram
- 2 to 3 dashes of Scrappy's Bergamot Special Reserve Bitters

1. Place all of the ingredients in a mixing glass, fill it two-thirds of the way with ice, and stir for 30 seconds.

2. Strain over a large ice cube into the double rocks glass, garnish with the dehydrated lime wheel, and enjoy.

AME SOEUR

Another life-changing cocktail from Camille Cavan and the team at Quaintrelle.

★

GLASSWARE: Cocktail glass
GARNISH: Edible flower blossom

- 1¼ oz. cold-brew coffee
- 1 oz. Green Chartreuse
- 1 oz. coconut milk
- ¾ oz. Simple Syrup (see page 20)
- ¾ oz. Amaro dell'Etna
- Heavy Vanilla Cream (see recipe), to top

1. Place all of the ingredients, except for the vanilla cream, in a cocktail shaker, fill it two-thirds of the way with ice, and shake until chilled.

2. Double-strain the cocktail into the cocktail glass and layer vanilla cream on top, pouring it slowly over the back of a spoon.

3. Garnish with the edible flower blossom and enjoy.

HEAVY VANILLA CREAM: Place 1 cup heavy whipping cream, 1 oz. vanilla bean paste, and ½ cup Simple Syrup (see page 20) in a cocktail shaker and shake vigorously until the cream is very thick. Use immediately or store in the refrigerator.

62 PANORAMA PUNCH

At Inside Passage, this drink is served in an actual 1962 Seattle World's Fair glass. Let this fruit-and-spice creation transport you to the World of Tomorrow.

GLASSWARE: Collins glass
GARNISH: Bay leaf, candied cranberries, scoop of mandarin & almond sorbet

- 1 oz. Trois Rivières Amber Rum
- ½ oz. Rhum Clément Creole Shrubb

- ½ oz. Copperworks Gin
- ½ oz. fresh lime juice
- ½ oz. cranberry juice

1. Place all of the ingredients in a cocktail shaker, fill it two-thirds of the way with ice, and shake until chilled.

2. Strain over ice into the Collins glass, garnish with the bay leaf, candied cranberries, and sorbet, and enjoy.

CONVERSION TABLE

Weights

1 oz. = 28 grams
2 oz. = 57 grams
4 oz. (¼ lb.) = 113 grams
8 oz. (½ lb.) = 227 grams
16 oz. (1 lb.) = 454 grams

Volume Measures

⅛ teaspoon = 0.6 ml
¼ teaspoon = 1.23 ml
½ teaspoon = 2.5 ml
1 teaspoon = 5 ml
1 tablespoon (3 teaspoons) = ½ fluid oz. = 15 ml
2 tablespoons = 1 fluid oz. = 29.5 ml
¼ cup (4 tablespoons) = 2 fluid oz. = 59 ml
⅓ cup (5⅓ tablespoons) = 2.7 fluid oz. = 80 ml
½ cup (8 tablespoons) = 4 fluid oz. = 120 ml
⅔ cup (10⅔ tablespoons) = 5.4 fluid oz. = 160 ml
¾ cup (12 tablespoons) = 6 fluid oz. = 180 ml
1 cup (16 tablespoons) = 8 fluid oz. = 240 ml

Temperature Equivalents

°F	°C	Gas Mark
225	110	¼
250	130	½
275	140	1
300	150	2
325	170	3
350	180	4
375	190	5
400	200	6
425	220	7
450	230	8
475	240	9
500	250	10

Length Measures

$\frac{1}{16}$ inch = 1.6 mm
⅛ inch = 3 mm
¼ inch = 6.35 mm
½ inch = 1.25 cm
¾ inch = 2 cm
1 inch = 2.5 cm

INDEX

ABOUT CIDER MILL PRESS BOOK PUBLISHERS

Good ideas ripen with time. From seed to harvest, Cider Mill
Press brings fine reading, information, and entertainment
together between the covers of its creatively crafted books.
Our Cider Mill bears fruit twice a year, publishing a new crop
of titles each spring and fall.

"Where Good Books Are Ready for Press"
501 Nelson Place
Nashville, Tennessee 37214

cidermillpress.com